SMILE

BEHIND THE LENS OF THE "DATING GAME KILLER"

RYAN GREEN

For Helen, Harvey, Frankie and Dougie

Disclaimer

This book is about real people committing real crimes. The story has been constructed by facts but some of the scenes, dialogue and characters have been fictionalised.

Polite Note to the Reader

This book is written in British English except where fidelity to other languages or accents are appropriate. Some words and phrases may differ from US English.

YOUR FREE BOOK IS WAITING

**From bestselling author
Ryan Green**

There is a man who is officially classed as "**Britain's most dangerous prisoner**"

The man's name is Robert Maudsley, and his crimes earned him the nickname "**Hannibal the Cannibal**"

This free book is an exploration of his story...

Get a free copy of ***Robert Maudsley: Hannibal the Cannibal***
when you sign up to join my Reader's Group.

www.ryangreenbooks.com/free-book

CONTENTS

Ready, Set, Flirt

The lights were blinding. It was something that they always said about being on stage or a film set, but you never really understood just how intensely the bulbs burned until they were focused on you. Cheryl found herself blinking hard just from walking out onto the soundstage, and they hadn't even put the spotlight on her yet. She hadn't understood why the girl backstage had slathered her up with so much makeup, but now she got it. It didn't just have to hold up to the scrutiny of everybody watching, it had to hold up to the blazing lights. The blush still had to look like a blush in the fog-light glare of the halogens. It would have taken all of that just to keep people looking human under the white shine.

That was only problem number one. Problem number two was that she was already starting to sweat through the makeup. She wished that she'd worn something less conservative so that she wouldn't roast under the lights like she was trapped in an Easy-Bake oven, but she was going to be on national television. She couldn't have people looking at her and thinking that she was... that way. It was bad enough that they were going to be making a joke about her massaging her boss, and her cleavage was pretty out there, even for the kind of fashion that was okay nowadays. And her hair, she loved her hair all feathered out and everyone said she looked amazing, but my god was it hot under here.

Going on a dating show like this, was already kind of embarrassing. Like she was admitting to the whole world that she couldn't find a guy for herself. She could. Of course, she could, she just had standards. And even if she didn't have standards, who wouldn't want a moment in the limelight? She was pretty sure that some of the contestants that had been on before already had boyfriends of their own, but they just wanted the whole world to see their pretty faces.

Well, why shouldn't Cheryl get her chance? She'd heard that some of the girls who went on these shows ended up getting jobs in Hollywood after folks saw how good they looked on the TV screen. Why couldn't that happen for her too? She deserved it as much as anybody.

Everything blitzed by in a confusing buzz. There were so many people all around her, that she didn't even realise that Jim Lange was right there at her side until a few minutes after he'd popped up and introduced himself. After his brief introduction, he seemed completely oblivious to her, standing on his marked spot on the floor, checking that the cameras were focused on him, and him alone. He was practising his smile, over and over again, staring into the camera. A little cock of the head and a grin, a signature move that she'd seen on her own television a million times and never considered was anything but natural. It felt wrong to be on this side of the screen. Like she'd fallen down a rabbit hole into wonderland.

There were cards in Jim's hands. The questions she'd be asking the bachelors. They'd all been read to her backstage before they started, while she was still in the makeup chair, then a clipboard with those questions had been pressed into her hands so she could read them for herself, over and over, so that she wouldn't mess up any of her lines. It was almost a joke. She'd be introduced by Jim, she'd ask her questions when prompted by

Jim, she'd laugh or nod or shake her head when the bachelors answered the questions with their own pre-prepared answers, and at the end, she'd pick whichever one of them had the nicest voice, because she knew that the answers to the questions didn't mean a thing.

Then the frenzy of motion all around her abruptly stopped. All the crew that had been scuttling around like an overturned anthill suddenly vanished back into the woodwork. The live studio audience – that the television had always told her the Dating Game was filmed in front of – filed in to take their seats in what looked like rickety metal bleachers. Then just as all the crew had faded away to nothing, so too did all of them, they'd barely been visible beyond the lights before and now that they were silent, it was as if she was all alone in the world, the only eyes on her the shining lenses of the cameras.

She was led offstage by one of the production hands and placed on the exact spot from which she would soon make her entrance. They waited as the music played, then Jim said "Good evening" and they went through the show's usual introductory spiel. It was so familiar that it almost felt like home, the same voice, the same music, but it was bigger and more real, not like the tinny sound of Cheryl's television set back home. There was no static buzzing at the periphery of her vision, no chance a strong wind might knock out the signal completely. This was really happening, she was in TV land with all these other TV characters, and if they liked her enough, she'd get to stay.

The different bachelors were all introduced and right off the bat she knew who she was going to pick, a photographer who liked skydiving? Nobody was going to top that, she couldn't even imagine all the excitement that he could bring to her life, even if it was only one date. She'd have a blast with that guy, and more importantly, it would keep her here, in the limelight, in the spotlight. A photographer would get her into Hollywood parties and know all the best people, this guy could totally change her life.

She didn't miss her cue, but that was only because as Jim was saying the word "Bachelorette", the production assistant grabbed her by the arms and bodily pushed her out in the direction of those damned lights once more.

She was blind in the first instant that she stepped out, only able to keep moving thanks to the practice runs they'd already put her through all day. She didn't need to see to know that looming shadowy figure was Jim Lange, any more than she needed to know the way to the upright stool where she'd have to perch herself like a prize on a pedestal all the way through the show. She'd tread the path a dozen times before, and the fact that this was the real Jim instead of his stand-in made no difference. She smiled for the cameras the way that she was meant to, never looking at them, only at Jim and the audience, so that everything seemed casual and fun. It felt like the false face that they'd plastered over hers might crack at any moment.

Then she made her first mistake. She wasn't meant to be going to the chair yet, she had to go and be introduced by Jim, to have a little witty repartee, to show everyone what a catch she was and why they should keep on bringing her onto TV. And right off the bat, she was already screwing up. She was tripping over her words, even as Jim told the embarrassing story about how she lost her job when one of the men had asked her for a massage, all she managed to muster was an embarrassed smile. Come on Cheryl, get it together, this is a live studio audience, there is no do-over, there is just here and now to get everything perfect, to make the whole world love her.

She'd missed some of what was being said after her moment of being flustered, but now she was being steered towards her little seat in the middle of nowhere and the cards were in her hands. She could do this. She remembered this from practice. From seeing a hundred other girls do it on TV, just the same.

Then from the other side of the divider, she heard his voice. "We're going to have a great time together, Cheryl."

It should have slowed the hammering of her heart but instead, it made it beat faster. It wasn't that he knew her name, or that he'd said it with such absolute confidence that he was going to win, even though she knew he was, it was something else, something she couldn't quite put her finger on.

She pushed it aside, took a deep breath, focussed on the questions in her hands. Remembered what she was meant to say. The other two introduced themselves too, but the buzzing in her ears as she quashed her panic drowned them out.

Then it was her turn to talk. She put on the voice she'd been practising in the mirror for weeks, the best TV personality voice she could muster, like the girls who presented the weather after the news, all accent stripped away, big enunciations of every word so that there could be no accusations of mumbling. "Bachelor number one, what is your best time of day?"

It was such a nonsense question, she'd be amazed if anyone could come up with an answer that actually made sense. It was like asking what your favourite colour was. A nothing question that told you nothing about the person.

"The best time is at night." Bachelor number one replied without hesitation. "Night time."

It sent a prickle up her back all over again. That same smooth confident voice. The subtle implications of spending the night with him and what that might entail. Trying to keep the conversation going instead of showing herself to be a total airhead on TV, Cheryl asked him, "Why do you say that?"

As if there was anything more to what he was saying than the same stupid double entendres they shoved into every episode of this show.

"Because that is the only time that there is."

It stalled her out for a moment, she'd expected a moment to think, a moment when he wasn't answering back in that same smooth voice. Charming and cool. She almost tripped over her words again.

"The only time? What's wrong with morning, afternoon?" She'd been given no prompting here, this was just her, wheels spinning hopelessly in the air on live TV. Her family was watching her. Her friends. And that was the best she could come up with.

"Well, they're okay, but the nighttime is when it really gets good."

She would have killed to have that kind of confidence. Even if what he was saying barely made sense, he said it so calmly that she caught herself nodding along. She pulled a smile like he was amusing her with his antics, even though the whole conversation was just weird, and then she moved on.

The others answered the same question with similar levels of nonsense, but her mind was still hung up on Bachelor Number One. She had already picked him out before she got on stage as the man she was taking home, but now she found herself almost intrigued. She wanted to crack through that smooth exterior and see what was really under there.

The next question, when the time came, was even more ridiculous than the first, but it also gave her the opportunity she wanted to make him crack, to break through that slick act and make a fool of him. "I'm a drama teacher, and I want to audition each of you for my private class." She wiggled her eyebrows suggestively, expecting a laugh from the audience and getting nothing. "Bachelor number one." She put on her best attempt at a sultry voice, "You're a dirty old man. Take it."

There wasn't even a breath of hesitation or surprise. "Come on over here." He let out a growl, barely human. Then another, deep and low in his throat. How could he take such a stupid thing and try to make it sexy? What was up with this guy?

She ended up making a fool of herself, trying to do an impression back as the crowd applauded his suggestive grunts. But she couldn't allow her shame to show. Just keep on smiling, like you're having the best time of your life. That's what they'd told her. No matter what, just keep smiling. The show must go on.

The next question managed to be even more coarse than the last. What kind of food would he be? Bachelor One said he'd be a banana, and when pressed for more details, he'd just replied that she knew why. Even though she knew that this was all staged – that the men had probably been given lines to read just like she had – she couldn't help but feel like the lines they'd fed Number One were the most repugnant. She was still going to pick him because she had to pick somebody and the others sounded like a snore-fest, but she got the distinct impression that he was the kind of guy who was only after one thing.

They went through the rest of the show and she managed to say all the right things and smile just right, earning some approving nods from Jim as they went along, which made her feel certain that she had a bright future ahead of her in show business. She finally felt like she had her feet under her when Bachelor Number One came strolling around the divider to meet her and her stomach dropped.

It wasn't that he was a bad-looking guy. Quite the opposite. He was handsome and charming, and he put an arm around her as though they'd been dating for months to put on a show for the cameras, but all the time that they were being told about the fabulous trip that was planned for them, to an amusement park, she could feel the weight of his arm around her and the heat of his body against her. Hotter than even the studio lights and her feathered hair. She could feel sweat prickling all along that side of her body, and the nausea that she'd earlier attributed to nerves just kept on worsening the longer that they were in close proximity. They walked off the stage together, with his arm still vice-like around her and he smiled down at her with absolutely nothing behind his eyes. A shudder ran down her spine, but that just made him smile wider. She tried to politely pull away, but he wasn't letting his prize slip out of his grip yet, instead leaning in for a kiss.

That was enough. She put a hand on his chest and held him off, mumbling something about waiting until after their date. The production crew had been basically ignoring them up until that point, but now blessedly, one of the many gofers came scurrying up to start talking over the details of their prize and when they'd be able to claim it. That was enough of a distraction for her to slip out of his grip, and by the time that they were back to their respective dressing rooms and her heart had stopped thumping wildly, her mind was made up. She wasn't going anywhere with that guy. He was setting off her creep alarm, loud and clear. When the production assistant came by to get her to sign off the final paperwork for their free trip, she declined.

The PA looked confused, to say the least. The whole reason most people came on the show at all wasn't to find love but to get a free holiday out of the deal, but Cheryl insisted. She didn't want to go on a date with that guy, she didn't even want to be in the same room as him again. Something about him was wrong, and she didn't want to hang around him long enough to find out what.

Begrudgingly, the PA finally took her at her word and went off to break the news to the rest of the team. It sounded like there was even more argument breaking out just outside her room. Cheryl didn't care, they couldn't make her go on this date, it wasn't like they filmed them going. There was no reason that they had to push her. She just wanted this whole thing to be over. Sure, the PA had made some noises about her being "difficult" and how nobody wanted to work with difficult women in the industry, but at this point her mounting anxiety about the whole thing had overtaken any silver screen dreams she might have been harbouring. She could hear a man shouting now, somewhere off in the building. Yelling her name. She didn't budge from the spot. If it was that creep Rodney from on stage, she didn't owe him any explanations. If he'd wanted to date her, he shouldn't have been such a weirdo the whole time. Just barely, as the guy was being hauled off out of the studio and she was cowering in her dressing room, she heard him say her name again, faint as a breeze. A promise, or a threat. "I always get my woman."

Rodrigo

Rodrigo Jacques Alcala Buquor was born on August 23rd, 1943, in San Antonio, Texas. Under the law of the time, he was considered a citizen of the United States as both of his parents were residents there, and he received his birth certificate from the local notary. His parents were Mexican-Americans, Raul and Anna-Maria Buquor, and little Rodrigo was the third of four children that the couple would produce over the span of their unhappy marriage. Against the wishes of Anna-Maria, Raul made the arrangements for the whole family to relocate back to Mexico in 1950 when their little boy was only seven years old and had barely started making friends in school. The whole family was uprooted, all sense of stability stolen from the children as they went from their childhood home and the steady rhythms of their father's drinking and working, to Mexico where it seemed that all of the rules and structure that they had lived by were now entirely dissolved.

Matters did not improve as time went on. Their father, already prone to a wandering eye, would vanish for days at a time, leaving their poor mother alone, with no money, to fend for the whole family in a country that was unfamiliar to her after having lived most of her adult life in America. Anna-Maria did the best that she could for her family, but she had nobody around to support her and she did not know anything about the local systems that were in place that might have helped to keep their family afloat.

By the time that Rodrigo was ten, his father had vanished from their lives entirely. Raul Buquor had long been unhappy in his marriage, and the addition of all the extra responsibilities and pressures of being a father had made him ever more reluctant to come home each day. He did not have the courage to break off the relationship and face the consequences of this awful betrayal so, instead, he slunk away in the night without a word.

Anna-Maria was understandably distraught, but it did not take much more than one glance at her four children before determination took over. When they were lying in bed asleep, she could cry if she needed to, but in front of them, she would show nothing but strength. She had three girls sleeping head to toe in that little camp cot, and she would teach them that women could make it on their own without some useless man to support them. She would show the whole world that she was capable of anything Raul had done and more.

It took less than a year before she had raised enough money working odd jobs while the kids were at school to relocate the family back to America and the support network that she had built there. While most would have expected her to head back to the familiar territory of Texas, where her old friends might have been found, she instead swung west and headed out to California to take advantage of all the new opportunities that were opening up there. They found a home in the suburbs of Los Angeles, Anna-Maria found part-time work, and the kids were enrolled in schools as swiftly as possible.

It was then that things started to change for Rodrigo, now going by the anglicised version of his name; Rodney. He was reasonably popular at school, and the decently sized Hispanic population of Los Angeles in the 50s ensured that he was not singled out for bullying or exclusion just because he spoke

Spanish as easily as English. In fact, he was so light-complected that many people just assumed that his bilingual nature was due to a good education rather than heredity. That assumption of intelligence did not appear out of nowhere. Rodney was consistently at the top of his class across every subject. To his good fortune, he was never victimised as one of the "nerdy" kids because of his seemingly effortless academic excellence and he fit in well with his peers. In later life, his IQ would be tested by medical professionals, and they would discover that he scored around 135. Above the average by a large enough degree that the vast majority of things that most school children would have to work at were trivial for him.

It did not take long before he outstripped the limited capabilities of the public school that his mother had enrolled him in, and at their recommendation, he was put forward for several private schools that could provide him with the higher levels of education and stimulation that he would need. This turn of events evoked a great deal of fret and despair in Rodney's mother, Anna-Maria. She worried about the expected cost of such institutions but the alternative, to deprive her gifted child of the opportunities to fulfil his potential merely due to a lack of money, was both heart-breaking and unthinkable.

She was, happily, disabused of all these notions at the very first interview with a private school. They had no interest in taking money from her, they wanted Rodney to improve their testing scores. He was so smart, that they were willing to provide a full-ride scholarship. And in this new environment, Rodney excelled. He was popular, remained at the top of his classes, and even got to engage in a variety of extra-curricular activities that public schools could not have dreamed of offering. He was on the track and cross-country teams, but more importantly, he became involved in the yearbook planning committee, launching an interest in journalism, and more specifically in photography, which would come to determine the course of the rest of his life.

As the years rolled by, the many different schools that had initially offered Rodney their scholarship programs did not retreat, but instead made a competition of his choice of educational institution. Each of them would approach him with a better offer than the last; free equipment to use, access to more modern facilities and even the promise of a more active social life, and time and again, as soon as the offer became good enough to convince both Rodney and his mother, their lives and schedules would be thrown back into turmoil as a ten minute walk to high school became a cross-town bus trip, or vice-versa. Eventually, at the age of 16, Rodney would graduate from Montebello High School. But not as valedictorian as many in the faculty expected. His interest in academia had waned as he grew older, and increasingly his attention was focused less on his schoolwork and more on his schoolmates. Girls became his obsession. Every day, all day long, he was trying to chat up the girls at his school, to get their numbers, to fix up dates.

His mother used to laugh about her little boy trying to play Casanova, but the fact of the matter was, Rodney was pretty good at it. He learned from his mistakes, improved his flirting, and came back again stronger each time he was rejected. By the time he was leaving Montebello, he had dated the majority of the girls in his year as well as quite a few of both older and younger girls, too. Most of these relationships were short-lived because Rodney didn't actually know what to do with a girl once he'd gotten her. He had no real interest in building a long-term relationship or even much in the way of a friendship with most of the girls he pursued, it was as though he was acting entirely on some sort of hunter-gatherer instinct. Trying to "get" girls even though he didn't really know what he wanted to do with them once they were "gotten".

As he grew older and his hormones kicked into high gear, he went from being confused about his own desires to being entirely focused on them. The girls that he dated later in his high school career were not being selected for the excellence of their character or their beauty, but because of rumours that they were willing to "go all the way'" with boys.

As it turned out, the rumour mill was incorrect about the ease with which all of these girls could be bedded, and so Rodney became increasingly frustrated. Even those girls who had given up their virginity were not interested in jumping straight into bed with him – and given that this was literally his only use for them, he rarely got to that stage. Instead, he became incensed by their "rejection" and blew the whole date the moment that they resisted his overly amorous advances.

For such an intelligent boy, his animal impulses and emotions always seemed to get the better of him when finesse would have served better. If he had managed to conceal his true desires while faking his way through relationships, he likely would have gotten exactly what he wanted, but impatience always seemed to win out, and that left him bereft of the sexual release that he was so desperately seeking.

Despite all of this, his mother was still laughing about the young Lothario, telling him that one day he'd meet the right woman and settle down. Rodney did not feel this to be accurate. He had never met any woman that could hold his interest for very long. In truth, if the girls had just been willing to give it up immediately upon meeting him, he'd probably never even say a single word, let alone go through all the trouble of wooing and romancing them.

Soaked in frustration without an outlet, and confronted with the unfortunate reality that he had no idea what he was doing with his life, Rodney tried to seek out a place in the world. Somewhere orderly where everything made sense and he could get some of his pent-up aggression out of his system.

At the age of 17, just days after completing high school, he walked into a military recruitment office and joined the United States Army. He was recruited under the supposition that he would serve as a paratrooper, skydiving out of planes into enemy territory, but the reality of his service was markedly less exciting.

His capabilities were noted early into his career, and the military complex quickly identified him as someone who could be much more useful to them behind the scenes, doing paperwork and math that the average foot-soldier just wasn't quite up to the task of completing. Instead of a soldier, Rodney became a clerk. He was assigned to Fort Bragg in North Carolina, on the other side of the country and in the heart of the war machine, where most American soldiers trained, and through which the majority of materiel consumed by the army passed.

Worse still, he had absolutely no say in the matter. He had enlisted in the army expecting an escape from the boredom and drudgery that seemed to plague the lives of all the adults he knew, but all that he found there was more of the same bureaucracy. Fanning the flames of his discontent was the fact that he couldn't leave. This wasn't a job he could up and quit just because he hated it. When he joined the army he'd signed on for a tour of duty, and he had no way to get out of it. If he tried to walk out, he could end up in jail as a deserter, or worse.

So, he tried his best to keep his head down and keep on going. He filled out an endless litany of requisition forms and filed all the appropriate reports every time a shot was fired on the shooting range. A range that he was barely even allowed to visit in passing, let alone train at. He was miserable, and his luck with women was not improving.

While many of the men on campus had relatively successful dating lives outside of work, Rodney did not. His attempts at meeting up with local women were inconsistent at best, and he soon began to build up a disciplinary record as local girls came forward and accused him of sexually assaulting them.

The cases were all handled internally by the military police. The local police never heard anything about Rodney's behaviour, and the girls were too ashamed of what had been done to them to publicly discuss it. This gave Rodney free rein to offend again and again. Admittedly, he did receive as much punishment as the military was willing to hand out, but nobody in the establishment wanted to deal with the shame of a soldier behaving in such a manner, so all decisions were made behind closed doors, and the punishments that he suffered were for lesser charges than his behaviour warranted.

If Rodney had been the ideal soldier and behaved himself well, he would still have been miserable as an army clerk, but the reality is that he did not comport himself in accordance with the high standards that were expected of him. Beyond the constant complaints about his behaviour when he was off campus, his superior officers also noted that he was insubordinate to the point of belligerence. Ignoring their orders when the orders didn't suit him and taking petty revenge whenever the opportunity presented itself. His official file actually contained the word "vindictive", and he repeatedly lived up to that descriptor. He would rearrange material deliveries and deliberately mismanage the base assets to ensure that those who had crossed him or disciplined him would receive the worst duties, have no access to the luxuries they most requested and were generally kept as uncomfortable as possible.

The other word used to describe Rodney by his superiors was "manipulative" and it could not have been more accurate. Specific details of how he wrapped the other soldiers around his little finger are sparse, but he was reprimanded multiple times for encouraging behaviour that was considered unacceptable. Whether this was in reference to the sexual contact between soldiers, which would have been kept off the record, or in reference to the way he provoked infighting between various social groups, partly for his gain and partly for his own amusement, is unclear, but it was quite apparent that he was a disruptive element that the brass wanted to be rid of.

He was unhappy, his superiors were unhappy, the people he was manipulating were unhappy, the women he was sexually assaulting were unhappy, and nobody was pleased about the situation that they were in. The only way to resolve it was to remove the disruptive element, and the only way to do that was to find a reason to discharge Rodney.

So, they made life worse for him. His superior officers played the same game he'd been playing with all of them, finding out his least favourite jobs and assigning them all to him, increasing his workload until it would break the back of a normal clerk, and then marvelling as he managed to push through and get it done anyway. The army might have bragged about all their soldiers being exceptional, but in the face of a soldier who was actually exceptional, they had no idea what to do except turn up the heat even higher. For weeks, and then months, Rodney's frustrations grew. He was bombarded with pointless busywork and told to prioritise it over his essential functions until he was working late into the night just to keep his head above water. But as he suffered, so too did everyone around him. He escalated his manipulations and vindictiveness, sharing the misery with anyone that came into reach, and now when he did manage to scrape together a few hours of free time to go into town, he skipped past all the usual pleasantries and resorted to violently groping women and trying to physically drag them off – to the point that his fellow soldiers had to physically intervene to save them from his hunger.

Denied even this outlet for his mounting rage, it did not take much longer for Rodney to boil over.

He hit his breaking point three years into his tour of duty, in 1964. In the middle of his shift in the office, he stood up and walked out without a word to anyone. His co-workers glanced at one another in confusion, but nobody moved to stop him. Nobody wanted to get in Rodney's way, not with the way he lashed out. But when he didn't return for over an hour, his superior officer was finally informed that he'd abandoned his post. It was exactly the kind of mistake that they'd been hoping for. If he was shown to be in dereliction of duty they could begin moving towards a dishonourable discharge and be rid of the problem. All they had to do now was stand their ground and wait for him to come slinking back to his desk so that they could begin dressing him down.

Another hour passed, and there was still no sign of Rodney. The military police were contacted and asked to look for him, but after a thorough canvassing of the base, he could not be found. He hadn't just abandoned his post in the sense of leaving his desk, he had left the entire military base in Fort Bragg behind.

Once he had made it outside of the base, Rodney walked to the nearest highway and stuck out his thumb. He looked like a nice young man, so it did not take long before he was picked up. His usual charismatic persona had fallen to the wayside and he stared blankly out the window as his driver attempted to make conversation. That got him a fair distance, but he was making everyone uncomfortable enough by the time that they reached the state line that he was dumped out on the side of the road. He started walking in the dark of the night with his thumb out once again. It was harder to get a ride in the middle of the night, there was so much less traffic, even if every driver was a lot more sympathetic towards him. But by morning he'd ridden along with a couple of long-haul truckers that got him a little further along his way.

Some of them asked him where he was headed, but the rational part of his mind seemed to have gone silent and he could not say. Logically, he knew that there was nowhere for him to go, but he still felt that fundamental need to go, to run, to get away from the hell that he had been condemned to by his own stupid choices. He was sure there was a warrant out for his arrest by now, sure the police were chasing after him and that the minute he stopped moving they'd snatch him up and drag him back. Telling his drivers where he was headed would have been a bad move, even if he knew. It would have been leaving a trail.

But even without planning, some instinct was still guiding his motions. When he chose to go west at every junction, it was for a reason. He walked until his feet were bleeding and his legs were aching, just to get a little closer to the place he needed to be. When he saw the lights of LA rising from the horizon and he felt a swelling in his chest, it was because he felt like he was coming home.

When he made it back to the house that he'd grown up in and saw the light shining on the porch like a beacon, tears began to flow down his face. His mother opened the door to him, opened her arms and drew him in. She didn't care that he was AWOL, that he had blown his opportunity to make it in the army, she didn't care about any of that, just that her son was home and in her arms once more. All his frustration came pouring out. All the misery of the last three years of being bullied and bossed around by people who couldn't hold a candle to his intellect came pouring out.

He cried, they hugged, and slowly but surely, he found himself calm – but empty – inside. For the rest of that day, he went through the motions, helping out around the house in exactly the same way that he would have before he'd left school. He helped to put food on the table for his little sisters coming home from school and cleaned up in the garden, acting as though everything was completely normal, right up until the moment that the army jeep pulled up outside and the MPs came storming up the path.

He went without a fight, kissing his mother and sisters goodbye. The military police nestled him into the back seat between them, and they took off up the road back to Fort Bragg in the north of Carolina. All the way there, they talked to him, playing as though they were friends trying to get him to open up instead of prosecutors gathering evidence. It was ineffective. Rodney was entirely shut down, monosyllabic, a sharp contrast to the sharp tongue that he usually had when talking to them. It was like someone had flipped a switch and turned his personality off.

They wanted to bring him back to base and claim it was belligerence and insubordination that had driven him to abandon his station, to make an example of him to the other soldiers and bring everything in Fort Bragg back into balance with his removal. But they couldn't. He wasn't showing signs of having stormed off in a tantrum, he was showing signs of having suffered some sort of nervous breakdown.

He was confined to the brig on arrival back at the base, and fully expected to be dressed down by everyone up and down the chain of command. Instead, he was left in isolation. Left to stew in his own thoughts, completely unaware that he was being observed through a two-way mirror by both his superiors and the psychiatrist that they had brought in to examine him.

When the doctor came into the room, Rodney had no idea how to deal with the situation. If it had been someone in the usual uniform barking orders and damning him for his stupid choices, he would have risen to the challenge with the same anger that had carried him forward through so many similar clashes. Instead, he was disarmed by the situation, and when he started being asked questions, he didn't have the strength to lie.

As the day stretched on and they began talking their way around Rodney's problems, other tests were introduced and the observers were startled to realise that their free-range clerk was excelling at them. IQ testing was always conducted by the psychiatrist to determine whether a soldier was competent enough to understand what had driven their own actions, and typically in these circumstances the score was exceedingly low – explaining why they'd thought that they could just abandon their assigned tasks without consequences. But Rodney tested at the upper end of that spectrum instead. They couldn't eliminate him from the service due to a lack of intelligence and understanding of his actions, so they instead had to dig deeper and understand why he had done what he had.

The military psychiatrist eventually handed down a diagnosis to Rodney and his superiors. Antisocial Personality Disorder. It explained his resistance to authority, his inability to correctly manage his impulses and the way that he treated the women who had the misfortune to cross his path. In short, he was medically incapable of performing the role that he had been assigned, and to put him on the front lines was to put a weapon in the hands of a man who could kill without remorse, but also without discernment. The kind of man who might turn and shoot one of his fellow soldiers just because he felt the urge. He received a medical discharge despite his actions entitling the army to push for a dishonourable discharge. Attitudes about mental health were not very enlightened in those days. Once again, the US army was more than willing to sweep the ugly truth under the rug in order to avoid bad press.

So, Rodney was returned to his dear mother's care with a folder of notes explaining all the details of his "mental deficiencies" that he never elected to pass along to his own doctor, and he was at a loss for what to do with himself. He had hoped that the army might have given his life some purpose, or at least provided him with an outlet for all the anger that seemed to build up inside him every time he was confronted with the most minor of impediments, but that had been a dead end, just like his attempts to pair off with girls back at school. Sure, he'd had a little more success as an "adult" but even that had just been him losing his cool and grabbing at things that should have been offered to him freely. He didn't get it. He was good-looking, he was charming, and women should have been throwing themselves at him, but something kept spooking them before he could close the deal. They'd get to a certain point when they were about to head off alone together, and the girls – they'd just stop responding. It felt like running head-on into a brick wall, like he was in some cartoon and there was a tunnel painted on the solid rock. He couldn't understand what was happening, didn't have the empathy to see things from their perspective and recognised that his desperate hunger for them, even if it was reciprocated, was still off-putting. It made them think that there was only one thing that he was interested in. Which was, tragically, accurate. He wanted sex and nothing more. They wanted to imagine that there was romance and a relationship ahead of them.

Meanwhile, the girls who weren't above having sex just for the joy of it had enough experience with men to get the sense that there was something off about Rodney. Something that set their skin crawling and the hair on the back of their neck standing on end in those odd moments when he wasn't talking and putting on an act of normalcy.

It is a subject often joked about that one of the useful initial diagnostic criteria for assessing whether a person is a psychopath is the abrupt moments of discomfort that people feel in their presence. It is often compared to a prey animal's instinctual response to being confronted with a predator. A sense of dread, an inexplicable desire to get away, even if there is no rational reason or evidence to prompt that desire.

Surface-level relationships came easily to Rodney because he was all surface. He could chat with a person in a bar, make small talk, share details about his life and even copy the emotional responses that other people were having to certain stimuli, but beneath the surface, there was nothing there. All the usual questions that people would ask one another to get to know each other better came up blank for Rodney because he lacked the emotional depth required for dreams, long-term goals, or even the most shallow of relationships.

His life was at another crossroads after his stint in the army. With his medical discharge came a degree of respect that he had not expected. In fact, most people treated him almost like a veteran, behaving as though he had been injured in the line of duty rather than losing his mind and deserting his post because he was so incredibly bored with filing paperwork. Yet the question on everyone's lips was "What are you going to do now?"

For the most part, he lounged around his mother's house drinking. Not enough to make him a problem, but enough to make him an annoyance to her. She had already offered him all the support that he might need to do whatever he wanted with his life and his response had been underwhelming, to say the least. Knowing what he wanted to do was something that Rodney wasn't capable of. If two options were in front of him, he could pick without hesitation, turning his well-tuned brain to the task, but the kind of abstract thinking required to make life plans that could affect him for decades to come was more difficult to fake his way through with any degree of cleverness.

Reconnecting with some old school friends, he presented the problem to them, minus the parts about his mental health problems and women troubles. They provided him with a new framework for making decisions. On a bar napkin, they drew interlocking circles and explained that all the things that Rodney liked the most in life should go in the outer circles, and whatever job or lifestyle fit into the middle of the Venn diagram was the one that he should go after.

He pushed the idea aside while he was out with his ex-classmates, never sure exactly how much of himself it was safe to share with other people, but once he was back home in his childhood bedroom, he found a piece of paper and drew the circles just like he'd seen in the bar.

Women. He filled that one in without a second thought. He wanted women above all else. Other things might temporarily quiet his lusts, but he knew girls, or at least, sex with girls, was the ultimate goal in his life.

That was the easy one, the rest required considerably more effort. He sat for almost an hour dithering back and forth over options, trying to think of something, anything, that he really wanted in his life beyond that. This turned out to be an answer in itself. In the next circle, he wrote the word "Easy". Then he took a moment to chuckle to himself and write "easy women" where those two circles intersected. Which left only the third circle to fill in. He wanted his life to be easy and full of women.

Briefly, an image of his future flashed before his eyes, some old Padre version of himself, rolling out of bed for mass, but surrounded by bickering nuns every other moment of every other day, endless sisters and mothers. He amended the "women" circle with the word "hot".

An easy job with access to attractive women. That didn't narrow down his problem.You could find attractive women everywhere. God knows he'd tried to talk to women. Women in every walk of life, on every stretch of road. Women were everywhere, but they always had something more important to do than talk to him. He was a nobody. That was the problem he was trying to solve. He was a nobody so women had no time for him. Women didn't care what he thought about them. They didn't want his attention, and they felt no need to impress him. Communication was a one way street that always ended at the same roadblock. He was forced to put himself all the way out there, only to be rejected, while these women had queues of guys begging just to look at them.

He could feel the anger, the old heat of it burning under his skin, the frustration at the never-ending rejections, the frustration at a whole world that seemed to have been built to keep guys like him from ever getting what they wanted. It wasn't fair. He didn't want much from life, but for some reason, he had to go begging and crawling for it while these women, they could just get whatever they wanted for nothing. Anywhere, anytime. Hell, most of the pretty girls didn't have to work or suffer through getting married, they could walk into any agency and get booked as a model and live the high life on their looks alone.

That was the job he wanted. Look pretty and live the high life. Excitement and pretty people, living in the limelight. But he hadn't been born a pretty girl, he was a man, and that locked him out in the cold. Just like with his mother and his sisters, they were always whispering amongst themselves, always looking at him sideways. He knew his mother loved him She had shown it a thousand ways. That's why she was so happy when he went off to the army, that last reminder of the villain of her story had been tucked away out of sight and out of mind. She'd never love him the way that she loved his sisters. And he'd never get to live the life that he wanted with all the beautiful people in the Hollywood Hills. Here he was, stuck out in the suburbs of LA, never getting close to the Walk of Fame, and that would never ever change. Fame wasn't for people like him. He hadn't been born beautiful. Nobody was going to see him walking down the street and discover him. Nobody would ever want to point a camera at him at all.

He blinked, sitting there on the edge of his bed, feeling somewhere between drunk and enlightened. The epiphany had hit him like a sledgehammer. Nobody was ever going to put him in front of a camera, but that didn't mean he couldn't be behind it. All those girls, all day long, desperate to make it, they all needed their pictures taken. All the magazines on the newsstands needed pictures of the rich and famous snapped. He'd been great with his camera back when he was working on the yearbook in school, and it had been the perfect excuse to talk to every girl. The perfect pick-up line, "You look like a model, can I take your picture?"

The enormity of what he'd just realised swept through him, driving the booze of the night away and leaving him, for the very first time, with a plan for the future. He could be behind the camera. He could go to Hollywood and find as many girls as he wanted, and every one of them would come chasing after him because in his hands he'd be holding the little lens that would let the world look through and see them. All the fame and fortune that every woman craved would be at his fingertips, and every girl that had ever turned up her nose or rejected him would come crawling back, begging him to do whatever he wanted with them, just so long as he'd take their picture and make them a star.

And they could all have their time to shine, he'd give it to them gladly, give them whatever they wanted. Just so long as he got what he wanted first.

He fell asleep that night with a big smile on his face and come morning his mother was shocked to see him up and about before her when she rose to get ready for work. The hungover wreck she'd expected to roll out of bed at midday was nowhere to be seen. Instead, he was bright-eyed, attentive, smiling, and spread out in front of him he had the university prospectuses that she'd been trying to force into his hands since his discharge from the army. All the possibilities, all the opportunities that she had never had and that he had been ignoring. Her face cracked into a smile as he told her about his plans, about remembering how much he had loved using his camera and working on the yearbook back in school. She was imagining him as a journalist while he was imagining himself as a pornographer.

The next semester rolled around, and Rodney was sitting at the front of the class in UCLA's photography program. He was so excited to be there that he'd barely slept the night before. Moving further afield than LA didn't seem to have occurred to him. UCLA had the best photography classes in the country, as far as he could tell, and it kept him home, close to his mother and close to the unattainable dream just on the periphery of his vision everywhere that he went. The words HOLLYWOOD spelt out up on the hillside that his bus rolled by each day. With a support network in place and his moods tempered by the joy that he was now taking in his life, Rodney was able to function like a normal person for a while. His impulses, his desperation and his frustration were all still there, simmering just beneath the surface, but they could be kept submerged and contained as long as he only had to contend with minor or imagined slights rather than any truly genuine sources of frustration in his day-to-day life. It wasn't an ideal solution obviously, because nobody could pass through their entire life without ever experiencing stress of any sort, but it did mean that he was able to keep up with his admittedly light class load while holding down a part-time job. A part-time job that allowed him to move out of his mother's house and into a little apartment of his very own.

He'd invite everyone back there to "party" after class, but there were very few takers. Most of them had their own social lives that didn't revolve around Rodney Alcala, school, or his idea of a good time. Every once in a while, a couple of the guys and girls from class would go out for a drink afterwards and he'd tag along, but he was never the life of the party the way that he wanted to be. Even here, doing exactly what he wanted to do with his life, he felt like he was on the outside.

And that sense of rejection was enough to tip the scales from him barely managing to restrain his worst impulses to his letting them loose. All it took was that faint hint of a rejection to send him back into the spiral of rage and despair that had cost him his army commission and years of his life. His utter inability to regulate his emotions like a normal person did not result in an explosive outburst as might have been expected from a child – the mind of a psychopath is far more complex, even without the underpinnings of an internal life that others have. Instead, he felt as though he had simply removed yet another of the restrictions that he had placed on himself so he could pass as normal.

If he couldn't get what he wanted by acting like everyone else, then the time had come for him to start acting like himself. Completely and honestly like himself.

Coast to Coast

There is no real question that Rodney had committed acts of sexual violence before he began studying at UCLA. There was no paper trail thanks to the army covering his tracks to avoid trouble, but there were enough people who could recall what had happened and that the army had not convinced to remain silent. The girls who had suffered his assaults, for instance. It is also well known that sexual assaults and even rape are rarely reported by the victim due to the stigma associated with such crimes. This was something that Rodney had been quite reliant on in his early years when he was simply "going a bit too far" with his girlfriend of the week, and it is because of that embarrassment and blurring of lines, that he got away with markedly more than he ever should have without seeing the inside of a courtroom.

We do not have records of any sexual crimes committed by Rodney during his first year at UCLA in 1967, but that does not mean that none were committed. It is entirely possible that he was on a veritable spree after acquiring a private place of his own for the first time in his life, but because of the aforementioned lack of reporting on such crimes, we know little of his illegal activities at this time.

In 2021, a report was made leading to our knowledge of the first attack that Rodney made, chronologically. Many could have occurred before that date in July of 1968, but this was the first that we know for certain happened.

Morgan Rowan was sixteen years old, out for a night on the town at a teenage nightclub on the Sunset Strip. She was living in Hollywood at the time, brushing shoulders with the kids of the rich and famous every day, and nights like this let her live the other half of that glamorous lifestyle alongside her friends. She wasn't rich like them, but she could scrape together enough to pass for their equal during outings like this. But the big difference definitely showed up at the end of the night when everyone else was hopping into their cars and heading home. Sometimes she'd beg one of them for a lift, but every time she did, she got that sad look from them. The one that let her know that she didn't really fit in. That she'd never be one of them.

So, when she got to chatting with a cute guy, one of the students at UCLA who was down in the teen clubs that night scouting for new models for his photography, it wasn't just nice, it was a relief. Sure, he was a little bit pushy, dancing a little bit too close for her and feeding her lines about how pretty she was and all the pictures he'd like to take of her. How she could definitely be a fashion model if she wanted to. How he could help her get a foot in the door.

She didn't want all that. It didn't sound the least bit appealing. Sure, it was the kind of life that she might want someday, but right now she was just trying to live. Why would she get herself involved with a guy like that now? Seeing her reluctance and trying to keep the good vibes going, he offered to give her a ride when the lights went up at the club instead. They could go out and grab something to eat or drink and then he'd run her home.

That seemed like a much safer proposition to Morgan. Instead of having to beg one of her rich friends for a ride, she'd get home all on her own, and instead of having to commit to some sort of business relationship with this guy, they could just go out on a mini-date and get to know each other without the overwhelming music drowning out every other word.

The club turned on the lights, everybody started filing out, and when her friends asked where she was going, and whether she needed a ride, she could tell them that she had a lift already. This hot college guy was going to take her out, then take her home.

She left with a little bounce in her step, so pleased about how the evening was going. She caught up to the man and hooked her arm through his on the way to the car. He seemed surprised, but delighted, that she was so affectionate already. Mostly it was just her good mood spilling over, luck was on her side tonight. And to make matters even better: pancakes. The International House of Pancakes, to be precise. He was taking her there for their midnight snack.

Or at least that was what she thought was meant to be happening. Instead, they seemed to be heading away from the main roads where IHOPs usually sprung up like mushrooms and headed out into what looked like a residential area. He pulled up outside an apartment block and turned to her with a grin, this was his place and there was already a party going inside. They could just sidle up the stairs and she could be in a real college party. None of the other girls had been to one. She'd be the coolest girl in school forever.

It wasn't what she had planned, but she trusted her luck. Everything was going well so far and this guy seemed to like her. It would suck to call a halt to all this. It would suck to call a halt to all this just because he wanted to hit up a party instead of eating pancakes in some all-night kiddie restaurant.

He was an older guy. He was mature. Of course, he wanted to do more grown-up stuff, and she was mature for her age too, he'd told her so, and that meant that going to a party after the club was exactly the kind of thing that she should want to do. The butterflies in her stomach as she climbed the stairs to his apartment were just excitement, not trepidation, and the fact that there was no music playing in his apartment when he went to unlock the door didn't mean there wasn't a party happening. He said he was a student, maybe they were all sitting around talking or something. That's what grownups did at parties, wasn't it?

But there was nobody there in the living room when he opened the door and the lights were out, and this wasn't a surprise party so it wasn't like there would be people hiding behind the sparse thrift-shop furniture.

She turned to ask the guy what the deal was, and he rammed into her with such force it knocked the air out of her lungs. His mouth was on hers. His foot was kicking the door shut behind them, jolting her sideways before he regained his balance. His hands were on her back, and when she flailed trying to pull out of the gross wet kiss with way too much tongue that he was giving her, he caught onto her arms instead. Dragged them down, pinned them to her sides and then twisted to pin her against the door.

This wasn't cute, this wasn't hot, he was being so gross right now. He shoved her back into the door and she banged her head on the little metal thing that covered the peephole, and then her hand was free, and she could get it against his chest and push with all her strength to get him unlatched from her lips.

It took way too much effort to get him off her, and she was so intent on that, she didn't notice him locking the door behind them. She tried to stop him, tried to say that she wasn't like that, that she wasn't ready to do all the things he seemed way too intent on doing, but she never got a chance. His hands trailed across her arms where he'd been holding her and to her chest. She let out a cry of dismay, but that just left her mouth open for a fresh tongue invasion. She couldn't believe that she'd once thought this guy was cute. This was so nasty. She just wanted to go home and use a whole bottle of mouthwash to get the taste of his mouth out of hers. Stale cigarettes and beer. Yuck.

Even now, she didn't recognise the danger that she was in. Even now she was treating it just like some schoolboy pushing his luck with her. She had no idea what she had just walked into.

The exact moment that she knew that she wasn't just in trouble, but in real danger was probably the first time that he hit her. She had started to struggle against him, trying to get away. It didn't work. He was so much bigger than her, so much stronger. It was a shock to realise that he could just pick her up and move her wherever he wanted. That she was like a child to him, or a toy. Once he had realised the same thing, he carried her through to the bedroom. All attempts at romance and kissing entirely abandoned, and his hands raked over her body relentlessly. Nausea bubbled up inside her the first time she felt his hand on her bare skin, and it only got worse as he dragged her clothes off and climbed on top of her. She screamed, she scratched at him, she did everything in her power to make him stop, but he didn't. When she hurt him in her attempts to escape, he hit her back, but otherwise, he just went through the motions of it all. Like his path was preordained. Like the part of him that did the thinking was no longer in the room. On animal instinct, he tore away her clothes, and on animal instinct, he pushed his way inside of her as she sobbed and begged for him to stop. He did not stop, he would not stop, there was nobody behind his eyes. There was no good nature she could appeal to, nor was there a bad nature that she could reach. There was a hollow vacancy in his eyes. He had the eyes of a dead man.

Somewhere amid the rape, there was a great clamouring outside. Banging on the apartment door. Shouting and screaming. Morgan screamed back, hoping against hope that somebody could hear her and call the cops. The whole thing was so surreal, only made worse by the flashing light. She had no idea what it was the first few times. She was trying so hard not to feel anything, trying not to know anything, to escape into her own head, away from the awful thing that was being done to her. It made her blind to everything; she could just sink down into the darkness and pretend that this was all just some awful nightmare if it wasn't for those damn lights blinding and blazing.

It wouldn't be until much later that she would understand what the thunderstorm she had been experiencing actually was. The flash of Rodney's camera.

The yelling and thumping at his front door had gone on climbing in volume, and with a grunt of disgust, Rodney pulled himself out of her and hauled up his pants to go yell at whoever was causing the ruckus and spoiling his fun.

Morgan lay there in shock, staring at the ceiling, with no idea in her head as to what she was meant to do now. Normally things were easy, everything followed after the previous action, but what was happening to her, what had happened to her, it was so out of context with everything that she knew of life that now she felt completely untethered from reality.

Which was why when she turned her head to the side to look out at the night sky and one of her classmates was right outside the window, it didn't come as a surprise. They were out there, the girls who had come to the nightclub with her, and their boyfriends. All of them, except for whoever was still hammering on the door, had come up the fire escape to this window, and now they were wrestling to get it open from the outside.

Dully, Morgan's eyes drifted over the frame to the latch. If that was open, her friends could come in. She pulled herself slowly upright, trying to drag her tattered clothes back around to cover her. The ache between her legs was like fire, like nothing she had ever experienced before. Every step that she took was a fresh agony, the jolt of her heel hitting the floor shooting up into her injured private places like a red-hot poker. But still, she kept on moving. Ignoring the yelling going on beyond the bedroom door, ignoring everything except for that latch on the window. She reached up for it and missed. Her hands felt numb. Her motions dizzy and clumsy. It was like she was drunk; maybe punch drunk from the beating he'd given her when she wouldn't give herself up freely. She fumbled at the latch again and again, until finally she got the metal hooked on her finger and she was able to yank the locking mechanism open.

In the next moment, she was completely encircled in arms. The girls. The girls she had gone out with that she was convinced had thought they were better than her. All the rich starlets in the making, they hadn't just come to save her, they were weeping with relief now that they had their hands on her. They were bodily carrying her out of the room, away from the nightmare that she had just experienced. There was not a single moment when someone wasn't holding her hand or cradling her in their arms, all the way back home.

She didn't feel safe again. She would probably never feel safe again for the rest of her life. Not fully. But her friends were there for her when nobody else could have been. They had worried about her going off with some guy, they had followed him home, and when it became obvious that something bad was happening inside his apartment, they had fought for her like knights in shining armour. She wouldn't have had a clue what to do in that situation. She still didn't have a clue what to do, but the girls she had been doubting were even her real friends at the start of the night had shown up for her, they had done everything that they could to protect her, even when it was her own stupid mistake that had put her in harm's way. They even helped her sort out her clothes and did her makeup to hide the bruises before she went back into the house. They told her it was her choice who she wanted to tell about what had happened that night, and they wouldn't share anything without her express permission.

The incident was never reported to the police, so Rodney never faced any consequences for his actions. Each time that he raped and beat a girl, he got away with it. Nobody seemed to notice, nobody seemed to care. He was finally getting what he wanted, whenever he wanted it, without consequence. He could hardly believe it. All this time, all he needed was the tiniest hint of power over others, the tiniest spark of celebrity, and he inherited everyone in Hollywood's immunity to the law.

40

The number of women that he lured back to his apartment in LA will never be known, but a few notable victims from this time period still stand out, in particular the one that resulted in his self-enforced exile from California.

Tali Shapiro was eight years old and living at the Chateau Marmont Hotel with her family. The place was like a fairytale castle, and it made her feel like her life was some sort of fantasy too. Living in the endless sunshine of Hollywood where the rich and famous passed you by in the street every day. It was a place so unlike everywhere else in the world that it felt like the normal rules didn't apply. It felt like the kind of place where anything could happen. And on the morning of September 25, 1968, something did happen.

As Tali was walking to school, a car pulled up alongside her, and the man inside called out to her, offering her a ride. Some part of her wasn't taken in by the glamour cast over this place, some part of her still remembered the lessons she'd been taught about going off with strangers, so when she was offered the lift to school, she turned it down. She peered in through the passenger side window at the long-haired man, and she didn't recognise him, so she said, "No thank you," and tried to carry on her way.

The man didn't take no for an answer. Just smiling instead of getting mad and explaining that she was smart not to get in the car with a stranger, but he wasn't a stranger, he was a friend of her parents, and they'd asked him to pick her up. Tali believed it. The man said it with such conviction and kindness that it didn't even cross her mind that he might have been lying. She hadn't really experienced any adults telling her lies at this point in her life. More importantly, the PSAs and campaigns that taught children not to speak to strangers didn't really get their feet under them until the 1970s. In the late 60s, there was still a sense of community and trust that would eventually be obliterated by stories of men like Rodney in the news. But for now, the world was a beautiful, trusting place, and little Tali climbed into the car without a backwards glance.

The man never said his name, but he chatted with Tali like she was a grownup. Like the things that she had to say actually mattered to him. It was another unique experience for the little girl. When he was telling her how pretty she was, that made her feel good too. It made her feel grown up to be having conversations like an adult would, and it made her feel proud of herself, that one of her parents' friends would come out and compliment her like that without any preamble or prompting.

They pulled up outside an apartment building, and she was a little confused about what was going on. She thought that the man was meant to be taking her to school. He was going to, he told her, but first she had to come inside. He was a photographer, and there was a picture that he'd shown her parents that they'd said she'd like to see.

When she asked what it was a picture of, he told her it was a surprise, and gave nothing more away. The whole thing had been mildly exciting up until now, but a twinge of anxiety about being late for school took her by surprise as he introduced this mystery. On the one hand, she desperately wanted to know what this picture was, but on the other, she didn't want to get in trouble. The man told her not to worry, driving was a lot faster than walking and he'd still have plenty of time to get her to school on time after she'd seen the picture.

She followed him into the building, glancing back at the road and the car reluctantly as they went. It was at this moment that another motorist rolled by the relatively quiet street and saw Rodney Alcala bringing a little girl into his apartment.

For the driver, Donald Hines, this set alarm bells ringing, and as soon as he was able to stop, he went to a payphone and called the police to inform them of what he'd seen. He didn't know Rodney, didn't know the first thing about him, but something about the scenario had left Donald feeling uneasy.

Meanwhile, Rodney led Tali into his apartment, through the living space, which still looked catalogue-perfect, and then through to the bedroom, where he kept his photographs.

He went over to a cabinet to look for the picture, but Tali could hardly see anything in the dim room. She looked around on the wall, covered in other taped-up photographs, and found a light switch. The single bare bulb hanging above the room bloomed to life and she turned back around to see how the man was getting on.

Rodney had found what he was looking for, but it wasn't a picture. It was a length of metal pipe. He brought it around almost casually, like a baseball player trying to bunt the ball. It hit Tali in the side of the head, and everything went dark again.

If she had been lucky, it would have stayed dark. But the world, the beautiful dreamlike world that she was so taken with, it would never come back. Instead, what she opened her eyes to was something so much worse. Her head ached where the bar had hit her. One of her eyes wouldn't open all the way, so that whole side of the room was shrouded in even deeper shadow, but what she could see, she wished that she couldn't. The man was there, looming over her, the light blinding bright when he moved aside, like a needle lancing right through to her aching brain. His face, she couldn't make it out anymore, he was a shadow, a silhouette, like the monster in a dream. But this wasn't a dream. She couldn't wake up from this. She tried to push herself up, to get back up off her back and to stand, to run. Her body didn't seem to be answering when she was calling. Her motions were slow, sluggish, like she was far away, shouting to her arms to move, to push. The metal bar that she'd lost sight of now came back into her vision in a blur of motion.

A kinder man might have hit her in the head. To knock her out. To make it stop before things got worse. But instead, he hit her across the chest and the ribs. She felt something crack. When she tried to breathe it burned. Her breath had been knocked out of her by the blow, and now it would not come back. If she'd had the chance to, she might have cried out, screamed, begged anyone in the world to come and save her, but she could not get the breath to do it.

Tears flowed freely now, blurring her sight even more. The shadow man moved around her, pacing around. The searing light stabbing at her again and again as he moved. His hands on her, they hurt less than the light until he splayed his palm on her bare skin and pressed down. Then she felt her broken ribs begin to move, digging into her from the inside, the jagged edge of it cutting inIt drove out the scream she didn't know was still inside her.

Her voice didn't sound familiar. It wasn't her. It was an animal sound, a retching sob. A wail born of pain. No wonder she'd never heard it before. She'd never been hurt like this. She'd never even known that you could hurt like this.

It earned her another blow from the metal bar. This one glanced off the shoulder to hit her in the cheek. Her jawbone cracked, her mouth drooped open and useless. Even her tongue flopped out the side like a dead slug. The pain was even worse somehow, sharper and fresher than the unbearable crunch of her ribs.

His hands were on her again, digging into her skin. Her clothes, she didn't know where her clothes had gone. The pain, the darkness, they'd stolen time from her. Enough time that he'd undressed her, underwear and all. Shame burned through her, but she was so confused and lost by now that having this stranger see her with nothing on was almost an afterthought.

Terror finally caught up to her. Until now, she'd been too disoriented to even process what was happening. To understand what was being done to her. The time that he took admiring his work, his eyes raking over her bare skin, gave her a chance to think. But thinking was not her friend at that moment. Thinking meant realising not only what had already been done to her, but what might be done next. She was too young to understand sex, the subject had never even been broached, and she'd lived a sheltered enough life to have not even the first inkling about it, and that ignorance truly was bliss. At least she didn't understand the full significance of what was happening when his blunt fingers pushed inside her, sending new awful pain burning up through the core of her to meet the throbbing of her ribs. Joining together to make a new incomprehensible total-body agony.

Even if she could have spoken, and begged him to stop, he wouldn't have. But he seemed to take her silence as compliance. He bent over her and pressed a kiss to her bare skin. She struggled then, seeing that sign of love twisted into something that it wasn't. She sobbed and tried to scream, even though air still hadn't made its way back into her and her lungs were burning not only with the broken bones pressed against them but also the absence of the oxygen that was meant to fill them.

It was a pathetic, feeble display of resistance, but it was all the resistance that the shadow needed to rain down more blows on her. Again and again, the metal bar rose and fell. The light above her strobing with its motion. Her own vision fading to black and then the fresh pain dragging her back up from the void where she might have found peace and rest. It all hurt so much, but he wouldn't let her go. His fingers were digging into her hips as he pulled her across the carpet towards him, but he didn't care that he was hurting her. He didn't care about her at all. The monstrous shadow only cared about getting what it wanted.

Over the course of almost an hour, Rodney Alcala systematically beat and raped the eight-year-old girl. It seems likely that he would have continued to do so were it not for the arrival of the police at his door, responding to the call from Donald Hines about Rodney's suspicious behaviour.

They hammered at his door and Rodney's eyes darted back and forth. From the girl lying stripped and beaten bloody on the floor to the door of the apartment, locked behind him, but not liable to hold up against any attempt to break it down.

All this time, he'd been doing whatever he wanted without consequences, and now the consequences were literally on his doorstep. He crossed the room in a few strides, dropping the metal rod he hadn't realised was still in his hand, and then he yanked open the same window that Morgan Rowan had escaped through just a few months before.

He hadn't known what he was going to do before his body was already in motion. The idea of abandoning his hard-won home and fleeing would never have occurred to him if he was thinking rationally, but his instincts were intact. The base drive that was inside of everyone, no matter how warped or twisted any other part of their mind might have been. Fight or flight.

Violent and sadistic as Rodney might have been, he had never been much of a fighter. He certainly didn't think that he could take on the cops at his front door, let alone the whole LAPD that would surely come after him should he manage such an unlikely feat. Animal instincts might have been in control of him, but that didn't mean that he'd lost all reason. He couldn't win in a fight, so the only other option on the cards was flight.

He took the fire exit stairs two at a time and made it down to the alleyway and out into the street without the cops upstairs even knowing that he was gone. Only then, as he made it to the end of the alley and stepped out into the light, did his rational mind take over again and slow his pace. A running man was notable, a guy going for a walk was commonplace. He'd always been able to blend in by behaving like everyone else. Mirroring their actions and their words to seem like he was a normal person. He wasn't normal, he had no desire to fit in with the crowd or pass as normal, but it was a tool that he could use to get by. To become invisible. After he'd made it a few blocks away and slipped beneath the oily surface of the crowds that he found there, he flagged down a taxi and headed further off into suburbia where he'd be even more invisible.

The police didn't break down his door, not when the building super was right there in the basement with a master key to every apartment, but once they laid eyes on what was lying on the floor of that apartment, the officers both wished that they had kicked it in the moment that they'd arrived. That girl, that poor little girl, looked like she was dead when they got inside. It was only when they checked her pulse that they realised that, somehow, she was still alive and breathing. An ambulance was called, and an APB was sent out for Rodney Alcala. The man was a monster. To do this kind of thing to any woman would have been horrific, but this girl wasn't even a teenager, she was just a child. And judging by the blood streaming down her thighs, it wasn't just the beating that she'd have to contend with if she ever woke up again.

The EMTs arrived before the detectives, but there was no way that they were going to keep the victim trapped there by procedure, waiting for cameras to capture her lowest moment. She was transferred to a stretcher with her neck in a brace and taken to a hospital. If there was any hope that she might survive, it was worth the loss of evidence at the crime scene. Besides, it wasn't like there was any mistaking what had happened here. A grown man had lured a little girl into his apartment, beaten her to the verge of death and raped her. Any other details were inconsequential. Even the weapon that had been used was still lying there, stained with smears of her blood. Bloody fingerprints still showing clear as day.

Tali Shapiro remained in a coma for over a month following her encounter with Rodney Alcala, and even after she woke up, she was not herself again. There were countless surgeries, blood had to be drained from where it was pooling inside her skull to prevent permanent brain damage. Everything that had made her the lovely little girl that she had been was wiped out, along with every memory of what had happened to her.

That was a small blessing at least, even if it robbed the police of any testimony that they could use to nail the bastard who had done this to her.

As for Rodney, he spent a few days drifting around LA, sleeping rough and skipping classes until he felt like the initial storm had passed by, then he went right back to his apartment to check if it was being staked out.

As it turned out, it wasn't. The police had kept watch for him there initially, but when he didn't return within a couple of days, the LAPD couldn't afford to keep burning overtime pay. He stepped back into his apartment, cleaned up the mess the police had left behind, and went on with his life as if there wasn't a warrant out for his arrest.

He returned to university and handed in all the required work, even passing his examinations without any real issue. He hadn't chosen the subject for its difficulty, after all. But when his time at university was done and he needed to move on, he found his wheels spinning again. He had been enjoying university life. He didn't feel ready to leave it behind yet.

What he did feel ready to leave behind was the feeling of constantly looking back over his shoulder and needing to duck his face away every time a police car rolled by. He needed to get out of LA, at least until his misbehaviour had been forgotten.

So really it was the perfect time for him to proceed with the next stage of his career. He had all the grounding in basic camerawork that could land him a job somewhere in Hollywood already, but his sights were aimed a little bit higher than just sitting behind a camera for the rest of his days. He knew that the real money – and the real power – came with a director's chair.

He knew that his real name had a warrant on it now, but it was an easy enough thing to change up some documentation before he sent it off to New York University.

His mother was heartbroken of course, utterly distraught that he'd be leaving the nest and crossing all the way to the distant east coast, but she also knew that there was an opportunity here for her boy to grow up at last. To be a man on his own terms instead of hiding behind her skirts. Going to New York was going to make a world of difference to the boy, so grudgingly she gave her consent, and no small amount of her savings, to see that it happened.

Of course, Rodney wasn't going to leave LA, his golden land of opportunity, without taking one last opportunity to sate his appetite.

On the 14th of February 1969, just before he departed for New York, Rodney took a drive down to Riverside County, taking in the natural beauty of California one last time before he headed off to the grim grey world of New York City. And lo and behold, he found even more beauty just by the side of the road while he was down there. Monique Hoyt was fifteen years old and hitchhiking on that fateful morning, trying to head home after a trip with friends.

When Rodney pulled up with a big smile on his face, he was a blessing, and the fact that he was so charming and chatty made Monique not only relax but actually start having a good time. She was old enough and worldly enough to know not to trust any older man showing too much interest in her, but this guy seemed to genuinely be an interesting person, less focused on trying to win her over, and more on just getting along with her. That helped a lot with keeping her calm when he pulled up in front of his apartment instead of taking her home like he'd promised. He said he just had to go up and grab something, and invited her to come in while she waited instead of sitting in the car, there was nothing untoward about any of it. Not really. He was treating her like a normal person instead of being a creep, and he was already doing her a favour so it wasn't like she could demand he do it for her faster. She trailed up the stairs after him, still chattering away as if they were friends.

It kind of felt like they were friends, that was the weird thing, she'd only known him for about an hour, but it felt like he was somebody who went to school with her. Someone that she'd known for years and years. She was so comfortable with him that she didn't even think twice when he locked the door behind them, and he still wasn't trying any funny business, there was no leaning in to try for a kiss or any of that crap. Then, like a switch had been flipped, his mask of humanity vanished.

Grabbing hold of her, he dragged her through to the bedroom. He stripped her shorts off her, even as she kicked and struggled. With a hand clamped tight across her mouth, he raped her. Not even bothering to beat her helpless. Every time she struggled too much, he'd shift his hand up just ever so slightly and pinch her nose shut. That would make her writhe even more for a little while, but then, she'd fall still and he could do whatever he wanted without interference. This happened over and over during their time together in his apartment.

The apartment was nearly empty by this time. Most of his possessions were packed for the move. The police had seized his collection of photographs to use as evidence. He seldom returned to his apartment if he could avoid going there, knowing that a police car might cruise past his building just as he was entering or leaving. He slept in his car more often than not when he wasn't staying with his mother, parking somewhere secluded to avoid any possibility of crossing paths with the law. This place had become a liability, like the rest of LA. He couldn't relax here anymore; he was forever looking over his shoulder.

Even as he finished raping Monique, he felt the walls closing in. He had to get out of here.

All of the kindness and pleasantry that he'd been using to lure her this far had vanished, but now that his initial lust had been burnt out, he spoke again. He ordered her to get dressed. She complied, partly because she was desperate to be covered again and partly because she was afraid of what he would do to her if she disobeyed.

They walked back down to his car together, him with his camera slung around his neck – the thing he'd gone to pick up – and her with her arms wrapped around herself. There was one brief moment when they were out in the street where she saw the opportunity to run, to find someone else, to get help, but he was right there beside her. His hand resting on the small of her back. Such a gentle touch compared to what he had already done to her, but enough to completely consume her with terror and disgust. When he ordered her into the passenger seat, she got in without a struggle.

They were headed back the way that they came, back towards Riverside County, she couldn't even imagine what was going through that monster's head. Did he think he could just take her back to where he'd found her and everything would go back to how it was? She knew his name. She knew his address. The second she found another human being, the police would be after him. He was going to pay for what he'd done to her. She was going to make him pay.

At what felt like the last moment, he turned off from the road back out into the middle of nowhere where he'd found her and and headed toward Banning instead and not to any populated region. Having people nearby would make life too easy for her. No, he was taking her to the mountains.

Her guts were already a knot of aches after what he'd done to her back at the apartment, but now it was so much worse as her anxiety mounted. If he took her out into the real middle of nowhere and abandoned her, she might never find her way back out. There were stories about mountain lions up in the hills around Banning, hikers went missing up there. Was this his plan? Drop her there and let nature finish her off so that he'd never have to face the consequences for what he'd done to her? She couldn't look at him anymore, not after what he'd done, she kept her head down and her eyes to the side, and against her will, her gaze kept on being drawn to the door handle. All she had to do was pull on it and jump out. It would hurt, but she'd survive. All she had to do was hurt and she could get away from him. Unless she got really hurt, and then he could just come back and pick her up again. Throw her around like a ragdoll again.

If she broke her leg she wouldn't be able to run, even if she got the chance. If she broke an arm, she'd be even more helpless to resist him. The only smart thing to do was wait, even if it meant letting him take her out there into the hills. Even if it meant risking being abandoned. At this point, she'd take a mountain lion over Rodney.

They went up some old dirt tracks, well off the roads that normal people used, and then when they got out into what looked like the middle of nowhere, Rodney stopped dead and climbed out. Monique was frozen. If she tried to run now, there was nobody that could help her. She didn't even know where she was. She just had to endure for a little bit longer. Not think about what he'd done. As soon as he left her out here, she could find this track again, follow it back to the road, flag down a car. Somebody would stop for her; she was sure of it.

But Rodney wasn't done with her yet. They hiked for what felt like forever, not talking, not looking at each other, the monster just hovering behind her all the way. It was like something out of a nightmare despite the bright sun shining down on them. With her every step she could hear his step behind her. Every time she turned her head she glimpsed his shadow creeping along beside her...At least she could wake up from a nightmare. At least with a nightmare, there was some hope of it ending with no real harm done.

At another spot that she would have said was arbitrary, Rodney announced that they were stopping. She didn't understand why, but she still didn't dare to cross him. Maybe this was where he was going to leave her. Maybe the nightmare was over.

He ordered her to strip.

At first, it seemed so out of the blue that she didn't know how to respond, but then the tears came. Pricking at the corners of her eyes. All the pain and shame she'd been trying to ignore until now welled up and overtook her. But despite that, despite how sick to the stomach the thought of exposing herself to this monster made her feel, her hands still moved to obey his commands. She wanted to live, and if this was the only way to do that, then she'd do it.

He stopped her before she'd removed her underwear and with one hand on the bare skin of her shoulder pushed her down onto one of the flat stones atop the windswept hill. She braced herself for him to touch her again, to do all the same awful things that he'd already done. She closed her eyes and told herself that she could endure, even though in her heart she doubted that she'd last another minute.

But his groping hands never came. Instead, she heard the distinctive click and whirr of a camera. At once her hands came up to cover her bare skin, her chest, but she could hear the monster tut and sigh when she did that, so she let them slip back down to her sides. Again, the click and whirr. This was beyond embarrassing, worse than shameful, the idea of him walking around for the rest of his life with those pictures of her, able to look at them whenever he wanted, show them to whoever he wanted. It was enough to make fresh tears of frustration come pouring down her cheeks. But she still did nothing to stop him, because if he was over there taking pictures, then he wasn't here, touching her.

She opened her eyes, and the blinding sun came rushing back in. She couldn't see him, except as a shadow looming there. But she could hear the shutter clattering, again and again. He spoke softly, telling her how to move, which way to look, what expression to wear on her face. And she didn't even feel shame or anger now, just relief that this was all that was happening.

He kept on taking pictures and she kept on not being touched for a long time, and it was the best part of her day. The only part where she wasn't afraid. He wouldn't hurt her now, not while he was taking pictures. That would spoil how she looked. So long as she stayed pretty, she was safe.

Rodney took hold of her by the hair. She'd been so lost in her delusions of safety that, for a moment, she hadn't even been paying attention to how close he had gotten. He slammed her down onto the stone, then that same hand went down to tear her bra out of place, to rip at her underwear. She didn't understand why he was doing this. She didn't understand why he was only using one hand either until she heard the click and whirr of the camera again.

He couldn't want pictures of this ugliness? He pinned her down, climbed on top of her, and forced her legs apart. And through it all, the camera clicked and whirred again and again. Even as he was raping her, he was dragging her around like a doll to better catch the sunlight for his pictures, to keep his shadow from occluding any detail. Her torture, her misery, they were his subjects. It wasn't her beauty that he was trying to capture in his pictures, it was his desires. The photographs from before weren't what interested him, they were just the prelude, the "before" to the "after" shots he was taking now. You had to see how perfect something was before you could understand the blasphemy of defacing it.

When he had raped her before it had been almost perfunctory. Like he was doing what he knew that he needed to do, but now he delighted in it. Stopping and starting, pinching her nose and letting her fade out not when she struggled – because she had no fight left in her – but when he wanted her to be blank-faced and unconscious, and when he wanted to see her face twisted into a rictus of pain. The first rape had felt like it lasted for hours, but this felt like it was never going to end. Like he was going to keep her out here on the hillside, waking her and knocking her out, snapping pictures from one angle or the next. He did other things to her then, things that she hadn't even known people did. Forcing himself inside her in places that she didn't even know things could go. And when it elicited a sob of pain, he brought a rock down on the back of her head to silence her. It went on and on, switching positions, switching violations. And then just when she thought that it couldn't possibly go on anymore, it did. It was as though there was no end to his stamina now that he had her just how he wanted her.

It did finally end when he had all the pictures that he wanted and he had finished once again, but by then, Monique had entirely retreated inside her head. Anything could have been happening to her and she would barely have made a grunt of pain to acknowledge it. When she was ordered back into her clothes, she dressed mechanically, and when Rodney told her to head back down the trail, there wasn't even a single victorious moment when she realised that she wasn't going to be left out here and her death wasn't going to be by exposure. She couldn't even feel good that she had endured the worst that he could do and come out alive. To be able to acknowledge all that she had overcome would be to recognise what she had been through and doing that was something that would have completely destroyed whatever was left of her. She just went along with what he said, slipping back into the passenger seat without a word, holding her head up just enough that he wouldn't tell her to sit up straight again.

The car went through a three-point turn and headed back down the dirt track towards civilisation, but it didn't feel like salvation was any closer. It didn't feel like anything at all. She was gone.

The next moment that she truly remembered, she looked around and it was dark. Rodney was gone. Her breath came unsteady and she jerked around looking for him, expecting him to be there just out of sight, ready to punish her for her inattention. But he really wasn't in the car anymore. They were at a petrol station. He'd gone in to pay. She had just been sitting here, all this time, while he left her. Blinking once, then again, her rational mind still a haze, instinct finally kicked in to save her. She grabbed at the door handle that had been tempting her all the way up the hills, and she pulled. The door swung open. He hadn't even bothered to lock it. Her legs were still weak and unsteady. The tearing inside of her brought awful jolts of pain with every step, but still she got herself free of the car and ran.

She ran and she ran through the dark of night along the side of the highway, terrified that the moment he got back to the car and saw her gone he'd come chasing after her. Finally, a police car pulled up beside her on the side of the road, and she collapsed, sobbing into the arms of the cop who had been sent out to stop the "crazy lady running along the side of the road."

It wouldn't be until the early morning that she had calmed down enough to share her story. But the moment that the name Rodney Alcala left her lips, she saw every cop in the room stiffen. They knew Rodney. They knew what he was, and he had still been free to go and get her. It sent her into another spiral of sobbing and terror. Even if the police had been able to stop him, what hope did she have of ever feeling safe again?

Burger and Lies

New York agreed with Rodney in a way that he really had not been expecting. Where LA was this huge sprawling place, the Big Apple was compact, built on top of itself. There were so many people all crammed into so tight a space that they all seemed to end up completely blind to one another. Even riding the subway, crammed in like sardines in a can, most people never even made eye contact with one another. It was kind of remarkable, the invisibility that crowds granted him ramped up to almost supernatural levels with there being so many bodies all around him, and the New Yorker attitude of completely ignoring everything that was happening around them meant that even the people in the crowds weren't a danger to him anymore.

He found himself a comfortable apartment that was near to a subway line that ran all the way to NYU, and he was all set. Everything on this coast was in the name John Berger, which he figured was inoffensive and forgettable enough that it wouldn't draw any attention, and he'd been training himself to respond every time he heard the name John. Even if he didn't quite have the whole alias thing perfected yet.

After he'd settled in, he called his mother, asking her to mail him the university transcript that he'd doctored to ensure his entry to NYU, but that was not the topic that she wanted to discuss. The police had been to see her, Rodney had a warrant out for his arrest. She'd spoken to a lawyer and they'd managed to arrange it so she could pay bail and he wouldn't need to go to court until his actual court date, but it was a lot of money, and she really couldn't afford it, and what the hell had he done that got the police involved?

He managed to dance around that last question, thanking her profusely for her help in posting bail and ensuring that his bright career didn't come crashing to a halt just because of some silly legal nonsense. It was enough to shut her up for now. She'd hate the idea of her meal-ticket child losing out on an opportunity. She couldn't see the sneer on his face as he spoke to her. She couldn't know the contempt he held. Not just for her, but for everyone in his life. She would have died for him, and he hadn't given her a second thought from the moment that he stepped out of her house. Whatever relationship they'd had when he was younger, as more and more of his internal world was consumed by his anger and his lust, it had been eroded away by the time that he was a grown man. He did not return to California for his court date, his mother lost the bail bond that she had made, and it was not long before she was in a spiral of debt, but Rodney didn't care. He had everything he wanted and needed from her, and now he viewed her as nothing more than a nuisance. Something to be rid of as soon as possible.

NYU was everything that Rodney had hoped it would be, and he began studying film there in earnest, fully intent on a future as a film director and producer, after he'd worked his way up the ranks as an editor or cameraman. The West Coast schools had always boasted closer ties to Hollywood and drawn interested students with the promise of brushing shoulders with celebrity, but NYU had managed a coup the year that a young "John Berger'" began to attend classes. Their film course was being taught by none other than auteur film director Roman Polanski, who it seemed Rodney got on with very well. Whether this was due to shared interests, or a similarity in psychology, is difficult to say. Regardless, he greatly enjoyed studying under the man and was a good student by all accounts. The university environment seemed to suit him a lot better than the structure of military service, certainly. Not to mention all of the free time it granted him to pursue his other interests.

Sadly such a lifestyle didn't come without a price tag, and so it was that Rodney had his second brush with celebrity in New York. He was constantly on the lookout for work, especially now that his mother had essentially cut him off, and he found it was plentiful in the big city. He took an office job that was willing to work around his university class schedule at the Blue Cross Blue Shield Association, a health insurance company, and unknowingly found himself in the presence of exactly the same kind of predator as himself. Hilariously enough, the talents that rendered Rodney and his counterpart invisible also resulted in the two men completely failing to recognize one another. Richard Francis Cottingham, also known as the Times Square Ripper, or the Torso Killer worked in the same office as Rodney throughout his tenure with Blue Cross Blue Shield, and neither one of them said so much as a word to the other, despite both of them being active serial killers at the time.

His work at BCBS was not the only undertaking for Rodney at this time. During the summer months, he had secured himself a job at a children's summer camp in New Hampshire, where young children with an interest in the arts could go to learn more about the respective crafts that they might consider pursuing. With his qualifications, the hastily renamed "John Berger" was their first choice to teach kids photography, even if he lacked practical experience as a teacher, he had a vast portfolio of candid and posed pictures of women and boys from LA that convinced the camp directors of his honed skills.

Between the two jobs, Rodney was making plenty of money to pay for his apartment and education, but he had little beyond that for frivolity, and with all the hours that he was putting into work, he had basically no opportunity to sample the many beautiful women that he'd encountered in the city. It was a new font of frustration for him, that he was finally somewhere safe, somewhere where his ruse of being a fashion photographer wouldn't be easily disproven, and now he didn't have the time to do anything. No time to trawl bars or nightclubs, no money or energy either. Unless a woman fell right into his lap, he was probably in for the longest dry spell of his adult life.

So as he was walking back to his apartment and spotted one of the most gorgeous girls he'd ever laid eyes on, he was feeling particularly delighted. She was moving furniture into an apartment, struggling with every piece, and it was laughably easy for him to rush up and take a corner and suddenly be inside with her. In moments he was her new best friend in the city. The only New Yorker willing to stop and help out a stranger.

He quite happily told her all about himself, his big movie dreams and his fashion photograph portfolio. Teaching kids about art and learning from Roman Polanski himself. He held nothing back, beyond those things that would have made her go running in terror because he had no fear of her knowing all of these details that she could repeat to the police later after he was done with her. Because he had no intention of her speaking to anyone ever again when he was done with her.

Cornelia Crilley was twenty-three years old. Markedly older than the teenagers that Rodney had preyed on up until this point. She differentiated herself not only with her age but with her maturity and awareness too. She may have been grateful for Rodney's assistance, and his attempts to win over her trust were definitely working, but she was not so naive as to believe that a stranger with no ulterior motive would have involved himself so thoroughly in helping her move into her new apartment.

In her day-to-day life, Cornelia was a flight attendant for Trans World Airlines. She spent all of her time on her feet dealing with the intrusive glances and casual brushing touches of male passengers. It was like death by a thousand tiny cuts every single day, but with Rodney, he was keeping his interest concealed. She had barely even seen him checking her out, even when he would have had ample opportunity. His eyes seemed to pass over her the way they did the furniture, for the most part.

When the last of the work was done, he offered to run out and get them some takeout for dinner, and Cornelia was almost impressed at how smoothly he was trying to segue from helping her out into dating her. But she'd been prepared for this eventuality. She asked to take a rain check, since she was exhausted from moving house and just wanted to go to bed.

Usually, this was where the horn dog she was dealing with would have popped out and shown himself, asking if he could go to bed with her, but this guy didn't. He said it was a shame because he was having a good time and hadn't made a lot of friends in the city yet but that was as far as it went. He didn't even try to get her number – he couldn't anyway, her new phone wouldn't be connected for a few days – or give her his. That did surprise her. There weren't many men who would just give up the chase like that. It made her think better of this John Berger, even as it stung her that he didn't desire her badly enough to put in the effort.

It was actually just enough that she stopped him from leaving, saying that he was right, that she should really eat something before going to bed, maybe he should stay. That little bit of reciprocation seemed to have been all that John needed because his eyes now raked up and down the length of her body, ending on her lips, even as a sly smile crossed his mouth. It startled her and put her on the back foot for the first time all day. The sudden switch from nice guy to animal normally wouldn't have been enough to spook her, she'd seen it before so many times, but she realised her predicament now, alone in her apartment with a guy who was essentially a stranger, whom she'd just provoked with a clumsy flirtation.

He saw that look of fear crossing her face and his grin spread even wider.

Just as his victim selection had become simultaneously more sophisticated and more dangerous by picking an older woman who had some ability to handle herself, so too did Rodney's methodology change to something more than bare-handed fumbling in isolated places. 427 East 83rd Street was not a quiet apartment in a run-down block, it was central New York, the other apartments were all occupied, and every sound that he made was going to be overheard by someone. What luck that they'd already established a pattern of thumps and bangs from moving furniture around.

Instead of his bare hands, Rodney formed a ligature out of Cornelia's nylon stockings after he'd stripped them off her and used that to cut off her air and her voice. He did not need to bear down on her neck constantly to keep her under control. Using the tights, all he had to do was close the noose around her neck just far enough to keep a proper lungful of air from getting in, and she became the perfect plaything. Too disoriented to resist, but still aware enough of what was going on that he could take joy in her reactions.

She hovered in a grey void, with little details of reality passing by like ships in the night. A glimpse of her bedside table in the periphery of her vision. A brush of her bared skin against the carpet. The sharp shooting pain as he thrust inside of her again and again. It all faded away and returned in waves. The nylon cutting into her neck was the only constant, the pain, and the pulsation of her blood trying to force its way past, making her feel like her own heartbeat was tightening the noose. When she thought, vaguely through the haze of restricted breath and blood, that it was finally over, she was shocked out of the grey again. A flash, like lightning, illuminated the room. Then again. And again. A strobe light that showed the shadow of her photographer as he loomed over her. As he forced himself on her again.

While Rodney would choke her to the edge of death repeatedly throughout the rape, this time, he did not leave anything to chance when he was done. Usually, when his carnal urges had passed, his victims were relatively safe. His sexual drive was what led him to commit his crimes, and while he was capable of thinking rationally and behaving in a way that would protect himself afterwards, he was not particularly driven to violence once he'd completed his task. Violence got him off, so once he'd gotten off, there was no more use of violence for him. What luck that he did not have to do anything particularly violent this time, to be rid of a potential witness and prevent the creation of another city where he couldn't stay in peace. All that he had to do was tighten his grip on the nylons already biting into her throat and wait out the last twitching struggles as she turned first red, then purple, then stilled.

It had been so much easier than he ever would have imagined.

At this point, most men might have faced some sort of ethical dilemma over whether it was right to kill to protect their secrets, but Rodney was so far past that point that it was almost laughable to think that he would have a moral objection to anything. So long as he was sated, he cared nothing for what happened to other people. You might even go so far as to say that he didn't even believe other people existed. He was the centre of his own universe, and everything that happened around him was merely sensory input. Other people didn't have their own internal lives, they were toys for him to play with, tools for him to use or impediments for him to navigate. Despite his documented high level of intelligence, he still retained a small child's understanding of the world, without sufficient empathy to do more.

Regardless of his motivations or what led him to this point, the deed was done now, and after he departed from the apartment on East 83rd Street, nobody would discover poor Cornelia's body for quite some time. Her body would not be found until June 12th, and the crime would not be connected with Alcala until 2011. Forty years later.

Meanwhile, back in California, the local police had finally admitted defeat in tracking down their rapist and handed the case off to the FBI for further investigation. In response to this, the FBI expanded their search for Rodney across the entirety of the United States, adding him to the top ten most wanted fugitives list at about the same time he was murdering the unfortunate flight attendant. Wanted posters were made with his photographs and posted all over the country. The police could not be everywhere and, for obvious reasons, Rodney had cause to avoid their attention, but the citizens who saw that poster had far better odds of encountering him and passing the information back.

Summer arrived, and with it came John Berger's job at the arts camp in the Hamptons. It was as cushy a gig as he had ever encountered, teaching snot-nosed kids from rich New York families how to point a camera at squirrels, and he was thoroughly enjoying the comfort and safety of being out of the city and away from the hundreds of thousands of prying eyes that would have been on him on any given day. What he could not have counted on was that those same kids liked to send letters home during their weeks' vacation. They would traipse down to the local post office to send those letters, postcards, and photographs back to their parents, and every time that they were there, they walked past the big board holding all the posters of the FBI's most wanted.

Three of the kids recognized their tutor and camp counsellor up on the board and on arrival back at camp, reported it to the people in charge. At first, it was brushed off as some sort of joke, but it was not long before one of the staff who'd been reported to happened to have to visit the post office themselves. At that point, the police were contacted.

The NYPD dispatched officers to pick up Alcala and in front of the whole camp he was marched out in handcuffs. The organizers of the camp were mortified and had to put out a press release explaining the situation to the families of their campers, tanking their reputation permanently and almost guaranteeing that future generations of wannabe artists were going to be deprived of the formative experience of art camp.

As for Rodney, he was loaded onto a plane with a pair of FBI officers and extradited to California to face the outstanding charges against him for what he'd done to Tali Shapiro.

The courts had an airtight case against Rodney, with more than enough witness statements and evidence to ensure that he'd be seeing the inside of a prison cell, but what they did not have was Tali Shapiro. She and her family had moved to Mexico following her recovery, and they outright refused to return, even when they were told that their refusal might result in Rodney Alcala walking free. They would not force their daughter to relive her terrible trauma. They would not pluck her from the new life she had built or drag her back into that nightmare.

The evidence that the state held was all good, but without Tali's statement, the court would be running a risk. They could not charge Rodney with rape and attempted murder without the testimony of their star witness; indeed, their only witness to the events of that day. Instead, he was handed down the lesser charge of child molestation, to which he gleefully pled guilty in exchange for the promise of a lighter punishment. And as such he was sentenced to three years in prison, instead of the life sentence that the heavier charge would have carried.

At this time in American history, law and order were a hot-button issue.

As a result of this political hot potato, arrests had shot through the roof as police tried to placate their political overlords with improved enforcement statistics. With the net result was that every single prison in California was packed to bursting point. Prison overpopulation was evident in every single facility, to the point that it had almost become a running joke.

On the other side of the coin from the hard-line law and order movement, was an opposing force working towards prison reform. A prominent and outspoken left-wing political faction believed that the purpose of imprisonment was not to punish offenders but to turn them into functioning members of society. Overcrowded prisons were a sign of mistreatment.

The result of their political maneuvering was the "Indeterminate Sentencing Program". The concept of this program was simple. If the purpose of prison was to rehabilitate the people confined to it, then as soon as they showed that they had been rehabilitated, prisoners could be released on parole. This placated the liberal faction that truly believed that rehabilitation was possible for all offenders, while also alleviating some of the overcrowding issues in prisons. It also had the net effect of improving the police arrest statistics, as the revolving door of prisoners under Indeterminate Sentencing meant that the criminals that they had locked up the week before would be back out again and reoffending in no time. Ironically, it was most beneficial for the "law and order" politicians to have more criminals back on the streets, as it allowed them to show all that they were doing to fight crime, whereas if there were any real change to the amount of crime, the bloated arrest and conviction rates that they were so proud of would have been gradually declining.

Regardless, the result of Indeterminate Sentencing was that after only 17 months, Rodney Alcala was back on the streets, living with his mother just outside LA, and back to his old tricks.

Less than two months after he was released, Rodney picked up a 13-year-old girl – identified as Julie J in records from the time – when she was on her way to school, with the promise of a lift. He then proceeded to ply her with marijuana and alcohol until ultimately attempting to have sex with her. Ironically it was the possession of a controlled substance in the form of marijuana that resulted in a breach of his parole and his arrest rather than the fact that he'd been attempting to have sex with a thirteen-year-old child.

The kidnapping of Julie J did result in an extended sentence being tacked onto the end of his existing one, but thanks to our old friend Indeterminate Sentencing, he would only serve two years in total. Rodney was paroled in 1976 at the age of 33.

This would be the beginning of his real crime spree. The killings that would make him famous.

Always Get My Girl

New York had been Rodney's home for much of his adult life, and despite his being unable to complete his education at the university due to the unfortunate interruption of spending several years in prison, he still felt like his life was there, not LA.

He met with his parole officer in Los Angeles not long after his release from prison and somehow managed to convince the man to allow him to travel across the country despite his long list of crimes and his well-recorded propensity for being a flight risk. With permission to travel, he caught the next cross-country flight back to New York City to resume his alleged career as a fashion photographer.

Within the week he met with dozens of women, convincing them to travel with him to locations in the areas surrounding the city that he had already scouted out as having ideal lighting and backgrounds for fashion shots, and some racier pictures that some of the girls consented to, giggling all the way.

He also flung himself into the nightlife of Manhattan that he'd always been too busy to enjoy during his last stay in the Big Apple. From here he made more connections and met more people who could help his burgeoning career or his gradually swelling portfolio. One such connection was Ellen Jane Hover, daughter of nightclub owner Herman Hover. Ellen was pretty well-connected herself thanks to growing up on the periphery of the New York club scene, boasting Dean Martin and Sammy Davis Jr as her godfathers. Yet despite these connections, she had never used nepotism to land herself a cushy job in the entertainment industry. She had worked for everything that she got, as much as she was able to in a world where all the doors swung open for her, and when it crossed her mind to undertake a modelling career as a stepping stone to singing, dancing, or even the stage, all that she needed were some good shots of herself to send around to agencies and she could almost guarantee that she'd get herself a decent contract. Enter John Berger, LA fashion photographer and occasional visitor to her daddy's club. They made arrangements to meet up for a shoot on July 15th, and on that day she left her apartment in good spirits.

It was the last time that she would be seen alive.

Her datebook was found, with the name John Berger against the date of her vanishing, but the name meant nothing to anybody. There were no people of interest in New York by that name according to police records, no ex-convicts with a patchwork of sex crimes on their paperwork. Certainly nobody by that name who had travelled across the country with permission from his parole officer. It was as though Ellen had simply vanished off the face of the earth.

Rodney continued the same patterns of behaviour for what remained of 1977, spending the vast majority of his time on photography, or at least on picking up women that he wished to photograph. Eventually, someone on the force who was familiar with the Tali Shapiro case came upon the name "John Berger" and ran a check for the man for whom it was a known alias, identifying that Ellen had disappeared almost immediately upon Rodney's arrival in New York.

They pulled him in for questioning, and he admitted to knowing Ellen Hover, but despite their suspicions, there was nothing the police could do at that point. They could hardly arrest Rodney on suspicion of murder when they hadn't even found a body. At the moment, it was just as likely that old Herman Hover would get a call from Hawaii where his daughter had eloped as it was that she'd never turn up again. There was just no way to know.

But despite this uncertainty, there were elements within the NYPD who remained convinced of Rodney's involvement and given the lack of leads and the immense pressure to get this particular case closed, those elements were given free rein to continue trying to build a case against him.

To that end, they continued their investigation by trying to build a timeline of Rodney's stay in New York, starting with his arrival, which they could identify from the airline's records, and continuing on to plot out his movements from that point onwards.

They found the apartment that he had rented, interviewed his neighbours for any hint of untoward behaviour and found nothing of note beyond his usual comings and goings at all hours. Nothing that proved that he was up to anything beyond the usual work of a photographer. The timeline of his movements was murky from then on, some clients could be identified, explaining how he was able to afford to rent a place in the city and keep his car running, but beyond the few hours that they could confirm he was engaged in gainful employment everything became exceedingly hazy. Widespread canvassing would gradually put them in touch with a number of women who had modelled for Rodney, but while a few of them would report having felt something "off" during their time together the majority simply recalled him behaving as a photographer should. It seemed that whatever it was that Rodney was looking for in a victim, some of them simply didn't fit that profile. Either that, or he was becoming more adept at controlling his impulses and limiting himself to only a few victims that law enforcement had not been able to track down any information on.

This in turn suggests that as much of a savage as Rodney Alcala was at this point in his life, he never lost rational control over his actions. The dark impulses that drove him to rape and murder were not overwhelming him, he was choosing when to succumb to them. He was choosing to rape and torture and kill women when it suited his plans, not because he was an insatiable murderer unable to control himself.

Eventually, one of these many dangling loose threads pulled taut. A model that Rodney had taken out to Pocantico Hills, 25 miles north of New York was able to guide officers to the exact spot where he had taken photos of her. It was on the edge of the John D. Rockefeller estate, on a hillside overlooking the Hudson River. In itself, it was not so different from any of the other locations that Rodney had scouted out and used, but as the officers searched around the area after their witness had returned home, they made a grisly discovery. Buried underneath a heap of heavy rocks on the hillside, they came upon the distinct reek of a decaying human body. With more officers called out, they carefully cleared the rocks away, photographing every step of the process so that they did not taint any evidence until they discovered a woman's body in a state of advanced decomposition at the bottom of the heap. Scavengers and the passage of time had deprived that poor woman of most of her distinguishing features, but it was clear at a glance that she had been naked when she was abandoned there. It would only be later, with assistance from the coroner's offices and dental records that the police would identify the body as belonging to Ellen Hover.

Despite this discovery and the multiple connections to Rodney Alcala, there was still nothing more than circumstantial evidence. It made him the prime suspect in the case, but there still wasn't enough to make an arrest.

In 1987 amidst those mounting suspicions, Rodney returned to California to escape the heat.

While he had been able to make ends meet in New York with his photography, the competition in LA was much more fierce and he found that while he could still convince literally hundreds of women and boys to become a part of his ever-growing portfolio, paid work was much more difficult to come by. To keep a roof over his head, he found employment with the Los Angeles Times as a typesetter. While he would have preferred to be a photographer for them, there weren't any openings at the time, and he had no proven track record for anything other than fashion and glamour shots. Still, his talent was recognised and the paper wanted to keep him around, just in case the opportunity for him to advance ever did come along.

It was a busy time for the paper, with record sales on many days, because of the active serial killer being pursued in LA at the time. The Hillside Strangler was a synonym for evil at the time, a serial rapist and murderer who had started by murdering prostitutes but now seemed to be branching out to kill any woman he could find in LA. It would later turn out to be a pair of killers, Kenneth Bianchi and Angelo Buono, working together, but in '78 the case was still wide open and the police were chasing down any lead that they could.

Every death produced a massive spike in newspaper sales as the general public, desperate for information to protect themselves, turned to their usual sources for information. As such, it wasn't uncommon for Rodney to be working double shifts to keep the papers churning out at the required rate, sometimes even having to be effectively "on call" waiting for the latest copy to be delivered for setting. He was a surprisingly efficient worker when left to his own devices, but the periods of downtime led to him socialising with his coworkers, much to the dismay of many of them.

He would share pictures with them, pictures of young women, generally wearing very little to nothing. He was very proud of his portfolio, but the lewdness of some shots led his coworkers to be concerned about the burgeoning pornographer in their midst. One of his workmates would later recount how weird he found the whole experience, but at the time no one thought to report it. When asked why he had taken the photographs, Rodney had blatantly lied, telling his coworkers that the mothers of the girls had asked him to help get their modelling careers started. He had probably thought that it would set minds at ease about how young many of the girls seemed to be if his coworkers thought that he had parental permission, but it was such a bizarre detail that it served to make them markedly more suspicious.

Those suspicions would eventually come to a head when the police showed up at the paper's offices asking after Rodney, seeking to question him about the Hillside Strangler case as a potential suspect.

The police were making their way through every known sex offender in LA, interviewing all of them on the suspicion that one of them was the Strangler, but in Rodney's case it was quite simple for him to convince the cops that he could not have been responsible, given that he'd been in New York throughout the beginning of the killing spree. In itself, coming under suspicion for the atrocious crimes of the Strangler probably would have been sufficient to see him lose his job at the paper, but Rodney was arrested while at the police station and did not return to work. The scuttlebutt at the LA Times office was that they'd been employing the Hillside Strangler all this time, and every reporter was clamouring for more information regarding what had happened. The truth of the matter was considerably less exciting than a serial killer having been discovered in their midst. When the police had brought Rodney in for questioning, he'd been searched, and they'd discovered a bag of marijuana in his jacket pocket that he'd forgotten was there.

After a brief stint in prison for that, Rodney was back on the streets again, deprived of his steady employment at the Times, where in addition to missing work for several months, he had also failed to disclose his history as a repeat sex offender when being hired. He relied entirely on his income as a photographer to keep himself alive. He managed to secure the odd gig, but none of his jobs paid enough to let him stop hunting for more work.

Despite this constant effort, he still took the time to photograph more and more people for his endless portfolio. One woman interviewed years later would talk about that portfolio, that he shamelessly showed off when convincing her to model for him.

The portfolio that he showed was composed almost exclusively of nudes, with many of them being sexually explicit to boot, there were hundreds of young women, but also nearly as many young boys put into exactly the same compromising positions. If this woman had been up-to-date about the latest missing person reports in Los Angeles, it is possible that a great many cases would have been solved that day. But she knew nothing about these cases so despite her discomfort at the idea that pictures of her naked body might be brazenly shown off in the same way to some other potential model, she still took Rodney up on his offer to take her pictures. He was just that charming.

In the midst of all this, Rodney received a phone call from the popular television show, The Dating Game. He had applied to be a bachelor almost as a joke to himself, thinking that he'd never hear back from them after they'd done the most basic of background checks on him. But they never did any checks. They took him at face value and invited him onto the show.

He was seated first, closest to both the host and the bachelorette, and enjoyed his time in the spotlight immensely. While the other two were awkward with their lines and fundamentally unattractive to Rodney, he had no shame whatsoever. He was willing to say whatever bizarre or depraved things the writers told him to say. For him this was no different from any other day, saying whatever he thought he was meant to be saying to get what he wanted, acting like whoever he was meant to be to keep whoever he was happy. In a strange way, a psychopath like Rodney was a perfect fit for Hollywood. Capable of slipping on any mask, assuming any role, if it got him closer to his goal. While everyone appearing on the show might have held some vague hope of being recognised as a talent and offered future work in the entertainment industry, Rodney was the only one who would have made a good fit. Like any actor, he had made a study of people, their behaviour and mannerisms, so that he could mimic them perfectly. But while an actor used such study to improve their art, to entertain and amaze, Rodney used it as camouflage so that he could slip past people's defences unseen.

He was introduced to the world as a daredevil photographer who went skydiving and rode a motorcycle.

Over the course of the episode, it became clear to Rodney that he was going to be the winner of the competition for a date. As was right and proper, he was the best looking, the coolest, and he had all the best lines. It made sense to pick him. He didn't say as much to his fellow contestants, but he did tell them that he always got his girl. One way or another. Something about Rodney by this stage was so unsettling that the other two contestants on the show with him took note of it. They'd later describe him as strange, with bizarre opinions that set him apart even from the various oddities of television. He seemed to genuinely believe that he was winning over the woman on the other side of the screen with his antics, rather than simply following a script. Though of course, to him, every social interaction was just a script to follow. He also seemed to believe that the other two men were in some way jealous of the success that he was having with the woman. There were also some seedier implications to the things that he was saying, suggesting that he didn't just think this was a gameshow, but that he'd somehow be entitled to do whatever he wanted with his "date" if he did succeed. The whole experience of talking to him was bizarre, in no small part because of the way that he would talk to his costars as though they were friends one moment, rivals the next, and then switch tone and behaviour entirely when talking with members of staff on the show.

Regardless, when he did win, he descended on the unfortunate bachelorette with a bizarre sense of entitlement, grabbing ahold of her as if she was a new prized possession rather than a person.

Things only grew stranger after the shooting was over and they were all shuffled off backstage to their waiting rooms again while paperwork was organised. He tossed himself onto the sofa in the green room with a condescending grin plastered across his face, talking down to his costars as if they were particularly upset about their loss rather than just being a silly gameshow. At least they had the last laugh when a production assistant had to come in and explain to Rodney that he wouldn't be going on the date as planned because the woman that he had been manhandling didn't want anything more to do with him.

Despite his unsavoury behaviour, Rodney had shown signs of intelligence up to this point, but now he became weirdly unable to understand what he was told. He was the winner, so he should receive his prize. The unfortunate PA had to explain to him as if he were a child that they had no legal power to force someone to date him. But Rodney replied that he'd signed a contract. That they had to. He had agreed to come on this show with the promise of a date if he won. Why were they trying to welsh on the deal now? Back and forth they went, over and over, with Rodney obstinately insisting that they owed him a woman. That woman in particular. He'd come on here to get her, and now he wasn't leaving without her. Eventually, the PA had to summon a member of the legal team to explain the situation and politely ask Rodney to leave, but that too was met with a complete lack of understanding on his part. They couldn't change the rules now. He'd done everything they told him to do so they couldn't change things just because his date had second thoughts. She had signed a contract just like he had. She was obligated to go out with him.

Eventually, it became apparent that he literally wasn't going to leave unless it was with his date, so they had to resort to summoning security to escort him off the lot. He didn't fight, but he was overcome with rage, ranting and yelling all the way out about how they had cheated him, how they had lied to him, how they wouldn't get away with this, he'd get his own lawyer and come back and force them to give him what he'd won. It wasn't hard for everyone involved to understand at that point why the poor woman who'd "won" him as her prize didn't want anything to do with him.

Rodney wasn't entirely unfamiliar with rejection. Indeed he had spent many years as a teenager having no success with women whatsoever, but he had thought that he was past that now. He was a good-looking man, with a cool job and cool hobbies, and every woman he met should have wanted him. Didn't they know that? Couldn't they understand all that he'd done to become who he was? Didn't they know that he could walk up to any pretty girl in the street and tell her a story and get her out of her clothes and in front of his camera? He knew that he had to operate with some degree of subtlety to avoid the attention of the police, but he couldn't believe that standing face to face with him, the people at the studio couldn't see him for who he was. If they knew who he was, how could they treat him this way? He was entitled to that woman.

Yet despite his best efforts and all of the information about her that he'd been given by the studio, even when he went hunting for her out in the real world, she remained out of his reach. He wanted her and he couldn't find her, and it brought back all the bad memories from the worst time in his life. All the frustration when he just couldn't find satisfaction.

If he hadn't already been a rapist and a murderer, this rage would have pushed him over the edge. Instead, all it did was make him sloppy. He had been operating carefully up until now, choosing his victims with care, ensuring that he only took the ones that nobody would notice had gone missing and that couldn't be connected to him.

Throughout the remainder of 1979, he would take many victims. More than he had taken over the course of any previous year, but it would be decades or longer before they were connected with Rodney. Where before he had been slow and discerning in victim selection, now he seemed to have descended into a frenzy. The humiliation that he felt after being so publicly rejected had regressed him back to who he had been as a teenager when such rejections and humiliations were an everyday experience, but unlike the teenage version of himself he now had all the skills and understanding of a fully mature serial killer. He was no longer being protected by the military, or by his youth, but by his own actions. There would be no swathe of complaints about him sexually assaulting women who had rejected him because he did not allow anyone who rejected his advances to live after he was done with them.

Robin Samsoe was twelve years old on June 20th when a strange man approached her and her friends at Huntington Beach and asked to take their picture. Some of them thought it was fun and struck poses as if they were girls in magazines, but it didn't take long before the guy seemed to grow bored and bid them farewell.

Later that day after she had returned home, thinking nothing more of it, she borrowed a bicycle to ride to her ballet class. She would never make it to that class. The bicycle would never be seen again. Immediately there was concern over her disappearance. She was not the kind of child that was likely to go roaming on her own, nor did she fit the profile of a runaway. Her family life was good, she had many friends and did well in school and her extracurricular activities. Nothing about her suggested even a hint of rebellion, and the fact that her parents had so immediately entered a panic on her failure to return on time from her class told the police that she was not inclined to dawdle or go off with her friends without informing her parents. A tense week followed, with a search being conducted all around Huntington and the surrounding areas for any sign of the girl.

She was nowhere to be found, and eventually, the search had to be abandoned entirely when no hint of her could be found.

It would not be until a week later that the remains of Robin Samsoe were found. A park ranger encountered the broken corpse of the little girl in the Los Angeles foothills, miles from everything and everyone she had ever known. Police would later come to realise that her body had ended up there after being thrown off the Santa Anita Canyon road, further up the slope, tumbling down through the dust and rocks until it finally came to its end. Some might have said that it was a blessing that she had died before suffering so rough an abandonment, but those people would not have been privy to the coroner's report on what had befallen poor Robin before she was tossed aside like a used napkin.

She had been beaten, repeatedly raped, repeatedly strangled, and ultimately stabbed with a knife when her killer had grown tired of her. Judging by the state of decomposition, the only small mercy was that she seemed to have been in her abductor's hands for a matter of hours rather than a matter of days, so the tortures that she had endured had not persisted for too long. Although given that we are discussing asphyxiation to the point of helplessness, brutal rape, and intermittent beatings during both, one could certainly argue that enduring such a thing for any length of time was too long. Particularly for an innocent child who had committed no sin beyond existing in the world and being spotted by a monster like Rodney Alcala.

There was no question then that this had been an abduction and murder by some sort of sex criminal. Given the limited contact that little Robin had with strangers and the alibis that all of her family and friends had been able to provide, that narrowed down the list of suspects to the strange man who had taken her photograph on the beach the morning before her demise.

The girl's friends were interviewed by the police at length, and an artist was brought in to work from the description that they provided, eventually producing a composite sketch that closely resembled Rodney Alcala. None of the locals, or even the local police had any idea about the identity of the strange man staring back at them from that page, but there were other people in the world who had already crossed paths with Rodney, who could recognise him. So when that picture was sent out to all of the law enforcement officers in the surrounding areas, and gradually filtered out to people on the periphery of law enforcement, Rodney's old parole officer only needed to take one look at it before calling in his report. The Samsoe girl had been taken by Rodney Alcala, he had no doubt about it just from the picture alone, and when he was informed by the officers involved about the exact details of the crime he could not help but match up the details with what Rodney had done in the past. Every detail matched. He approached his target in a public place where she felt safe. He isolated her from her friends before abducting her. Even his camera and gear matched Rodney's modus operandi to a tee.

A warrant was issued for his arrest the same day.

The Many Trials of Rodney Alcala

Despite the picture that the sketch artist had pulled together, at this stage the police had no actual evidence that Rodney was involved in the death of Robin Samsoe. There was no physical proof that they could point to that would connect the two of them, and given Rodney's freewheeling freelance lifestyle, there was no way to lock him into any sort of alibi that could be disproven either. They arrested Rodney in July of 1979 without any attempt from him to flee justice. He had the usual smirk plastered across his face that anyone who'd ever crossed him would recognise. That look of absolute certainty that he was so above it all that he didn't need to concern himself with what was going on around him.

He offered up very little information when interviewed, but didn't demand a lawyer, thinking it would make him look guilty. In truth, he expected to walk out of the interrogation cell the same way that he had when accused of the Hillside Strangler murders, albeit without the mishap with the illegal drugs in his pocket. They had nothing on him, so they'd have no choice but to let him walk.

Rapidly the investigating officers came to the same conclusion. A thorough search of Rodney's car and apartment had turned up absolutely nothing. They needed some physical evidence. At best, all they had at the moment were previous convictions and the possibility that Rodney had bumped into the victim at the beach. They needed more than that if they wanted to jail him. Luckily for them, the judge issuing warrants that day completely agreed with them that he was their most likely suspect and considered it to be more than reasonable for them to search his mother's house in Monterey Park also.

They hoped that Rodney had concealed all of his evil behaviour beneath his mother's roof. They were sorely disappointed. Time was ticking down on how long they could legally hold Rodney without filing charges against him and if they didn't get something to directly connect him to the murder, they were going to have to release him. It was a race against time to find something that they could use, and it was a race that they were losing. Though they tore up poor Anna-Maria's house there was no smoking gun, no bloody knife, nothing at all that would place Rodney Alcala anywhere near to where the girl went missing or was eventually found. They were ready to abandon all hope when they came upon a little scrap of paper that would change everything. A receipt for a storage locker in Seattle.

As the deadline ticked closer and closer, the detectives reached out to their counterparts in the other city. A couple of uniformed officers were dispatched to the location from the receipt and tracked down the owner, showing a faxed copy of the LA warrant as justification for asking him to pop open the locker.

What they found inside would change everything. There were boxes upon boxes of photographs. All of them neatly organised and filed away. But while many of them were sexually explicit enough to rouse the officer's interest and concerns, they were not the key item that they found with regard to poor Robin

Samsoe. Amidst the other miscellaneous detritus, half covered by an old t-shirt, they came upon a pair of gold earrings. Earrings that matched the ones that Robin had been wearing when she went missing, but that had not been found with her body. This was the smoking gun that they were looking for. This proved that Rodney Alcala had killed her.

On hearing that his storage locker had been found, there was the briefest flicker of doubt on Rodney's face, but then he moved right into his next lie. Those were his earrings. He'd had them for years. In fact, he'd been wearing them on his television appearance, hadn't they seen him? He thought everybody watched The Dating Game.

It was a ridiculous suggestion, but nobody had the footage from the TV show available to immediately disprove it. The police pressed on as if he'd said nothing despite the fact that he did have pierced ears, something still unusual for a man even in 1979.

He was taken directly to jail and denied bail by the court, given the severity of his alleged crimes and his history of skipping town whenever he was being pursued for criminal matters. It did not matter how much money his mother offered to put up, or the lawyers she hired, Rodney would be remaining behind bars until his court date.

A date which rolled around quite a bit faster than most, thanks to the publicity and public uproar surrounding the death of Robin Samsoe. He would be in court early in 1980 to stand trial, and while his lawyers did a decent enough job in defending him, given how damning the evidence was, they were not able to overcome the relentless efforts of the Orange County public prosecutors' office to see justice done.

In May of 1980, Rodney was sentenced to death by means of lethal injection, with that sentence to be carried out the following month. Rodney was stunned into silence as he was taken from the courtroom. He had thought that he was untouchable, that he would be able to go on acting out his grim fantasies forever, but now he was being abruptly snapped back to reality.

Yet despite the shock that he'd suffered, he wasn't dead yet. Working with his lawyers directly and studying legal texts in his prison cell, Rodney was able to find sufficient evidence of a mistrial for them to appeal the conviction.

The fact that there was an appeal in place meant that the state could not press on with the execution as scheduled, so Rodney was returned to his cell, where he would remain until the matter was resolved.

During his initial trial, many character witnesses had been presented by both sides to attest to Rodney's personality and known behaviours, and amongst them were the officers who had arrested him for the rape and attempted murder of Tali Shapiro, who provided graphic details of what he had done to that other young girl and the crimes that he had been convicted of as a result of his plea bargain. This constituted a violation of his rights. Information about that unrelated crime should never have been brought to the jury's attention, and as such, the Supreme Court overturned the results of the original trial after lengthy consideration in 1984.

A new trial had to be scheduled, this one taking place in May of 1986. In exactly the same courtroom where Rodney's defence had been defeated the last time around, events began to play out almost identically. The same witnesses were called, the same information shared, and everything except for the damning details of his previous sex crimes were recounted to the court exactly as they had been six years before. And just as before, Rodney was convicted of his crime and sentenced to death.

Before he was even back in his cell, he had already put the next appeal into motion. So long as he could keep fighting the case, he got to live, and despite the dismal quality of life that he was enjoying in prison, he was still clinging to his existence with all the strength that he had.

In 1992, the California Supreme Court upheld the verdict from the second trial, but with nothing but time on his hands, Rodney had already moved on to the next step of his plan. He filed what is known as a habeas corpus petition. In essence, a demand that his jailer bring him forth to court and prove that they have a right to hold him and that no laws were being broken or rights infringed upon by detaining him. To everyone's surprise, including Rodney's, a United States district court judge upheld the petition, overturning his second conviction and demanding yet another retrial. This occurred in 2001 but was challenged by the courts, resulting in another two years of delays before it was finally upheld by a Ninth Circuit Court of Appeals panel. The reason for this particular appeal's success was that Rodney had not been allowed to call a witness to confirm his assertion that the park ranger who discovered Robin Samsoe's body had been hypnotized before looking for it in the location where she was discovered by a member of the LAPD's investigators. While this may seem entirely laughable, and about on par with many of the ridiculous things that Rodney would say during his third trial, the fact that he'd been denied the right to call a witness to support his nonsensical statement still constituted a breach of due process. He might have been talking nonsense, but legally he had a right to try and prove that nonsense to the court.

In between his second and third trials, Rodney had not been idle. After slipping in the shower and hurting his back, he had filed a lawsuit against the prison where he was being held seeking damages. He also filed a second lawsuit against them when they refused to meet his special dietary requirements. As he had no special dietary requirements to speak of, at least according to medical staff, this latter case was thrown out without a second glance. As it turned out, he wanted the prison to offer a low-fat diet so that he wouldn't lose his trim figure. It did not take long for the former lawsuit to be dismissed either, with the court flatly stating that water on the floor of a shower was an expected hazard that could not be considered negligent.

In addition to his many litigious excursions, Rodney filled his time with writing, producing a full book entitled "You, The Jury". In this book he claimed his innocence in the Samsoe murder, fabricating a case for another suspect, and self-published it, with the hopes of turning public opinion in his favour ahead of his upcoming third trial. It was not widely read.

There was one additional matter that came up during the wait for his third trial. Up until now, the passage of time had been a victory for Rodney. Every day that passed was another one that he got to live, and another day in which witnesses' memories faded a little more. Up until then, the longer he had delayed his trial, the better his odds of winning had become. But now, things changed for him abruptly.

With the passing of a new law, it was permissible to sample the DNA of all prisoners to see if it could be matched to outstanding cold cases. Rodney attempted to legally fight this sampling, as he had everything else, but the courts had no right to overturn the law, only to interpret how it was upheld. Rodney did everything in his power to resist the DNA sampling, but ultimately there was nothing that he could do to prevent it. The results were immediate.

His DNA matched the semen left at the scenes of four murders in LA. In addition to his semen being discovered on or in all four of the women, there was also evidence to be found pointing the other direction. Another pair of earrings that had been discovered in Rodney's locker still had traces of DNA on them from one of these murder victims.

Jill Barcomb was 18 years old when she ran away from home in New York and traversed the whole of the continental USA to start a new life for herself in California. She had big plans for her future, the same dreams that everyone coming to Hollywood had. Not very specific plans, admittedly. There was no step-by-step guide to being discovered and making a career for yourself as one of the beautiful people. All that she really had when she rolled into LA on a Greyhound bus were a few dollars in her pocket and the vague hope that somebody would look at her and see something so beautiful it had to be shared with the world. Just like everyone else on the bus. Just like everyone else in town. So of course, she was primed and ready for a predator like Rodney Alcala to come strolling along. He introduced himself as a photographer, just as he had to all the other girls before, showing her his camera, his portfolio, convincing her that she had nothing to worry about, that he was trustworthy, that she should get into the car with him and drive away from all populated areas for the sake of making a connection to somebody in the industry. Caution wasn't so much thrown to the wind as it was launched bodily off a cliff.

As soon as Rodney had her alone, his façade of civility melted away and he became every bit the predator, proceeding to strip her, rape her, and strangle her repeatedly using the leg of her jeans over the course of several hours before finally rolling her body up into a ball and dumping it in a ravine off the side of a road in the hills surrounding LA.

Because the body was not discovered until the middle of 1977, when Rodney had already travelled across the country in the opposite direction, returning to his life in New York, he was never interviewed regarding this particular killing, and for the longest time, poor Jill was considered to be one of the many victims of the Hillside Strangler, given the location that she was found and her cause of death. Yet when the duo behind those crimes were captured and broke under questioning, Jill was one of the few bodies that they did not lay claim to. She was left orphaned as a remnant of that far bigger case. Essentially forgotten by the justice system when it was believed that her death could not be pinned on a serial killer. If she was just another teenage runaway, then as far as the police were concerned, this was basically a death by natural causes, and without the potential celebrity of a serial killer attached, the case wasn't worth pursuing.

Bringing Rodney to trial for this killing proved to be more difficult than the prosecutors anticipated, given the evidence they had available to them. If he managed to secure a scientific expert witness to attest to the failings of the DNA testing system that the police used, then they would be left with only one other piece of evidence connecting him to the case. An eyewitness who had seen him picking Jill up. Typically a case will not proceed to court without evidence to support the initial connection to the case. But the prosecution lost the right to use their most important witness when he committed perjury in another case. There was now a genuine risk of Rodney getting away with this particular murder, assuming that he had a halfway competent defence lawyer, and that made the prosecutors nervous. Juries didn't like to split hairs. They liked things black and white, open and shut. If Rodney was getting away with one murder, they might be more inclined to reconsider his guilt in the others. Jill Barcomb represented a danger to the prosecution. A risk in their otherwise flawless presentation. But despite this, they pressed ahead with the charges. They would not allow him to dodge justice, just because some idiot witness couldn't keep their story straight.

Georgia Wixstead was a little further afield from Rodney's usual hunting grounds, suggesting that there might actually be a multitude of other victims that simply haven't been connected to him. Not only was her body discovered in her Malibu apartment, but the manner in which she had been killed completely differed from the usual strangulation that Rodney seemed to prefer in his later years. Rather, she had been bludgeoned to death with a heavy blunt object. It was almost a throwback to his early days when he had beaten Tali Shapiro into a coma with a metal rod. The prosecutors believed that Rodney progressed past this behaviour as he honed his skills at abduction and murder. Now they needed to take account of a far broader swath of killings if they wanted to eliminate Rodney's involvement in them. Some investigators believed that Georgia was in her late twenties and more capable of defending herself than some of his other victims. Perhaps this caused his change of tactics.

That idea was rapidly disproved by the discovery of another body.

Charlotte Lamb was 31 years old when she died. Older and more capable than Georgia Wixstead, but still overpowered by Rodney in exactly the same way as he had treated the teenagers that he usually preyed upon. She was not discovered in her own home, suggesting that she had at least been canny enough not to invite her murderer into her apartment, but was instead found in the laundry room of her apartment complex in El Segundo. Just like his other victims from this time period, Charlotte had been found raped and strangled before he left her out on display for anyone to find on the folding table of the laundry room. Like many of his later victims, Rodney adopted a ligature with which to strangle her, rather than relying on the strength of his hands. In Charlotte's case, he had found a shoelace on a shelf in the laundry room and made use of that. The narrow band of fabric cutting into the skin of her neck as much as it was asphyxiating her. When her remains were discovered, there was blood all around her neck in addition to the hideous purple discolouration of what had once been a beautiful face.

Her earrings had been found in the locker that Rodney maintained in Seattle, alongside those of Robin Samsoe. She was killed in 1978, almost immediately after the debacle of Rodney's Dating Game appearance.

The fourth previously unknown victim was Jill Parenteau. A 21-year-old woman who had been killed in her apartment in Burbank. Yet another California town that the police had no idea that Rodney frequented. In the 70's the idea of a serial killer was just being formed, but by the time Rodney's third trial came around in 2003, the whole pseudoscientific field of profiling had been created to try and form theories around the behaviour of these monsters.

And Rodney broke the rules. Serial killers were meant to have set hunting grounds where they would find their victims, but Rodney's territory seemed to stretch from one coast to the other. They were meant to maintain a specific methodology for the killing of victims based on a rich fantasy life that revolved around killing, and once again, Rodney seemed to completely break that mould. For him, the killing seemed to be a necessity rather than a desire. Something that he had to do to ensure that he did not face charges for the innumerable rapes that he had committed. But not the driving force for his actions. He did not kill for a love of killing in the way that documented serial killers did, yet he still retained a great many of the other defining traits of those monsters in human skin.

Psychopathy, sadism, and narcissism are considered the dark trinity of a serial killer's psychology. The childlike inability to recognize the humanity of others, the joy taken from doing harm to other people, and the self-obsession that overwhelms rationality. There can be no denying that Rodney was possessed of all three of these traits, and even that he enjoyed the violence that he wrought on his victims and the feeling of power over them that he clung to, even years later, through possession of his photographs and trophies. Yet the act of killing was not what made him happy. It was a necessary task to tidy up the mess he had made rather than being the sole purpose of the exercise as it was for most serial killers. In fact, it might be more accurate to say that Rodney was a serial rapist with a terminally brutal method of avoiding the police.

Regardless, the more that the psychologists tried to put Rodney into a box, the more he confounded them. There were times he showed overt signs of psychopathy, at other times he expressed clear indicators of borderline personality disorder, and throughout everything, his stories were peppered with enough ambiguity as to suggest a multitude of other schizophrenia spectrum disorders making it obvious that no definitive label could wholly encompass the individual known as Rodney Alcala. He lied. He denied having any memory of events where clear evidence showed his culpability. He spun complex webs of deception and misdirection and outright nonsense to prevent his execution.

His attorneys once again put together an impressive case during the run-up to his trial. The state intended to charge Rodney with all five murders together, but his lawyers insisted that this was prejudicial. In four of the cases, there was DNA evidence, essentially guaranteeing a conviction. In the case of Robin Samsoe, the case for which he was originally meant to be facing trial yet again, there was only circumstantial evidence. In much the same way that mention of his conviction for prior sex crimes had prejudiced the jury against him in the first trial, so too would the knowledge that he'd definitely committed four murders prejudice the jury into believing that he had also committed the fifth.

Unsurprisingly, the court was not swayed by the lawyer's arguments, choosing instead to proceed with a joint trial for all five killings, cutting down on judicial expenditure and also bringing all five cases to a close simultaneously.

Once again, Rodney's representation was diligent, fighting the combination of the cases to the Supreme Court in 2006, when it was finally overturned yet again.

In response to this, Rodney fired his attorneys, announcing that he would be representing himself going forward. In a normal case, he might even have had some success. He was highly intelligent and had devoted his entire time in prison to studying the legal case against him. Nobody could argue that he lacked the motivation to fight his case harder than any hired attorney. His life was on the line.

Unfortunately for Rodney, he had no response to four new cases that had just jumped out of the shadows and clubbed him on the head. He testified that he did not remember committing these murders, but this was obviously not sufficient to allow the court to dismiss these charges. In fact, the prosecution proceeded to provide another open and shut case against him for each of these crimes which he didn't even attempt to fight. The prosecutors might as well not have bothered doing all of their homework, because although Rodney was not pleading guilty, neither was he providing any sort of defence. All of the prosecution's fears about him being able to pick apart the Barcomb murder charge vanished on the spot.

One of the arguments against combining the five murders into a single trial was that it would overwhelm the defence with too much information. That the lawyers simply wouldn't have been able to handle the sheer volume of material that was involved in such a prosecution. And it was a valid complaint. The amount of evidence and paperwork involved in even a single murder case can be enough to occupy a lawyer full-time for years, and by combining five, they were essentially ensuring that Rodney's defenders would not have been able to address all five charges on an even footing. In the case of a private attorney, this could be remedied by employing legal aides and throwing more lawyers at the case, but Rodney did not have a private attorney, his were assigned to him by the state since he lacked funds for a private attorney, and there was no budget to hire him additional lawyers just because he happened to have committed a plethora of crimes instead of just one.

So needless to say, if there was too much for a team of trained public defenders to tackle, it was beyond overwhelming to someone like Rodney, who had no legal expertise to speak of and was operating off a combination of sharp wits and instinct.

Choosing to represent himself in court could conceivably have elicited enough empathy from the jurors that he might have been able to avoid the death penalty being sought by the prosecution, or at the very least, he may have been able to convince them to recommend that it not be handed down. Unfortunately for him, he could not resist the urge to make a mockery of proceedings from start to finish. Throughout proceedings, he had to be asked many times to stop chattering, treating the whole thing like a social event. Things only grew worse after the charges had been read out and the actual process of the trial advanced.

He called himself up as the first witness for the defence and proceeded to interview himself for hours on end, rambling on in a monotone when he was not putting on the deeper voice he had chosen to be his lawyer persona. Out of all the ramblings, only one vaguely coherent fact was introduced. He claimed that he was being interviewed for a job as a photographer at Knott's Berry Farm at the time that Samsoe was kidnapped. Something that the prosecutors actually did have to disprove before the whole matter could be resolved. As to the clear evidence that he had killed Samsoe – the earrings that he had plucked from her ears – Rodney insisted that they belonged to him and that he had even been wearing them during his television appearance in 1978.

Pulling footage from an old VHS recording, Rodney attempted to show himself on the show, wearing the earrings, but it was pointless. The quality of the recording was too poor to prove anything. Just to be on the safe side, the prosecutors interviewed his costars from the bachelor side of the show, and both of them categorically denied any possibility that he had been wearing big gold earrings during filming. It would have been so unusual for the time period that they both felt that they would have remembered or at least commented on such a thing, and neither had.

There was a written affidavit from Samsoe's mother describing the gold ball earrings perfectly, accompanied by the receipt of purchase from when they had first been gifted to the girl for Christmas. On one hand, the jury had the word of a man who to all appearances was completely unhinged, and on the other, they had a legally binding document from a pair of grieving parents.

As a part of his closing argument, after the prosecution had quite ably dismantled all of the nonsense that he had thrown up as a smokescreen, he played the song "Alice's Restaurant" by Arlo Guthrie. A folk song in which the protagonist tells a psychologist that he wants to kill. Needless to say, this did nothing to convince the jury of his innocence either, instead simply marking the end of the absolute circus that he'd just performed in the courtroom.

It is difficult, knowing what we know of Rodney Alcala, not to view the entire exercise of defending himself in such a farcical way as a deliberate move on his part. Whatever his flaws, he had always been uniquely adept at manipulating how others perceived him and given that the narrative at the time revolved around serial killers being very serious and intelligent, the possibility of him trying to play himself off as just a goofball has to be considered.

He may not have been making any particularly logical argument to the jury, but he was making an emotional one:

Look at me, I'm just an idiot, you can't possibly think that a goofy little jokester like me could have done all the terrible things they're saying I did.

If that was his intention, then he clearly had not accounted for the jarring contrast between the damning evidence provided by the state and the ridiculous stand-up routine that he was performing being read as disrespectful to his victims.

All that the prosecutors needed to do to puncture his balloon of comedy was to describe the facts of the cases. As much as he might want to caper and joke now, back when he had his hands wrapped around a little girl's throat, nobody was laughing.

The prosecution was talented, they had not only provided the facts of the case but helped the jury to empathise with every single one of the women that Rodney had hurt. He might have been there in the room with them, acting out his nonsensical one-man play, but the ghosts of the dead women were there too, the memory of who they were and what they could have been, hung over the chambers, making every one of Rodney's acts of self-degradation into blasphemy.

The jurors did not look upon his farcical behaviour as evidence that he could not have committed the crimes, but as a sign that he cared so little about the victims and the proceedings of the court that he was taking his opportunity to defend himself from these charges and choosing to make a mockery of the whole proceeding. He did not win them over.

At this point in the trial, it was as though someone had flipped a switch and the imbecile who had been on the stand-up until now was subsumed back into the far more serious and unlikable man that Rodney truly was.

Recognising that he may not be able to secure an emotional victory, he began doing what a lawyer was meant to do and attacking the facts. First of all, he pointed out that the additional four murder charges being brought against him could easily have been tried separately but the prosecutors had insisted on tying them together to present him as some sort of mass murderer and incense the jury. Then he began rattling through the police reports and details from memory. There were multiple lapses in the witness testimony, both in court and back when they were first being interviewed. One of the girls that had witnessed the mysterious photographer on the beach that the court had assumed was him had described a dark-skinned and overweight man. Other witnesses had disagreed on the clothing that he'd been wearing. Even the initial police bulletin for the killer of Robin Samsoe had described a perpetrator who was bald. Rodney took great delight in showing off his long curly hair to the jurors. According to Rodney, the police had found him, decided that he was their perpetrator, and then completely dismissed any information to the contrary. Instead of deducing who the killer was from evidence, they had selected evidence that suited who they had already decided was the killer. He would be the first to admit that the DNA evidence of the other charges against him were damning, but that was why they had been attached to this case so that they could damn him when they should have been able to look at the flawed case on its own merits. Ultimately, that was all that he wanted them to do, to look at the case on its own merits instead of assuming that he was guilty just because he had committed similar crimes. If they had any reasonable doubt that he had been the one to kill Robin Samsoe, then they had an obligation to find him not guilty. If they simply hadn't been provided with enough information that they could be certain, then they should also have found him not guilty, as it was the prosecution's duty to prove it beyond all "reasonable doubt".

He showed a surprisingly good grasp of the American legal system, given that he'd had no education in that area beyond what he had given to himself. But even this sudden burst of extreme competence wasn't enough to sway the jurors so late in the game.

As for the prosecution, their closing statement was simply to reiterate all of Rodney's crimes. Talking about how he had sodomised a teenage girl before beating her head in with a rock. How there was a bite mark around one dead girl's nipple that had been matched to Rodney Alcala's dental records. A bite that had gone so deep as to almost sever it from the breast. How he had sexually assaulted one of his victims with a claw hammer. How he had choked every one of the poor girls listed as his victims until they were on the brink of death and then resuscitated them because he wasn't finished toying with them yet. They didn't need to make any emotional appeals beyond reminding the world what kind of man Rodney Alcala was and what he had done.

The time that a jury took to deliberate on a crime was usually longer based on the seriousness of the time and the complexity of the case. Rodney's crimes had been repugnant, but straightforward. There was no question of his guilt regarding the four murders. Only the matter of Robin Samsoe remained.

Guilt might have weighed on the jurors if deciding that one charge would have made any difference to Rodney Alcala's fate. If they thought that swaying the vote in his favour might have resulted in the death penalty not being applied, then perhaps they would have. But with four murders already locked in with guilty verdicts, the fifth and final one seemed to be nothing more than the finishing touch.

There can be no question that he had successfully introduced doubts into the jurors' minds with his last-minute outbursts. Doubts about the veracity of the police's open and shut case against him and about the whole nature of the investigation. But there were some cold hard facts that he could not talk his way around. Robin Samsoe's earrings had been found among his belongings, and there was no way that they could have come to be there without him being involved in her murder. He had attempted to introduce reasonable doubt regarding his ownership of the earrings in his earlier farce regarding a television appearance, but he had failed to do so, completely and utterly. It would have gone far better for him if he had simply claimed that he'd never seen the earrings before. Allowed the jury to assume that they had been planted there by the police who were trying to pin the crime on him. If he had focused on disrupting the case against him instead of wasting so much time spinning nonsensical stories and making a mockery of the court, he genuinely might have been able to avoid the outcome that was rapidly approaching.

Somewhat inevitably, Rodney was found guilty of all five charges of first-degree murder. He had completely miscalculated the gullibility of the jurors and the court and had assumed that they would be as easy to manipulate as his many victims had been throughout his storied career as a serial killer, but now he would be paying the heaviest of prices for his miscalculation.

The jurors were not a naïve young girl that he could convince would have her reputation ruined if she told other people what he'd been doing to her. They were not impressionable teenagers who could be convinced to keep quiet about doing grown-up things. These were fully competent adults, and they knew a liar when they saw one.

The court was quiet when the time for sentencing arrived, everyone knew that Rodney had repeatedly dodged the death penalty before, but with five women's deaths on his record now, it seemed impossible that he would be able to go on getting away with it. There was no question in the minds of the people in court that he was going to be put to death, and even those who opposed the death penalty could not help but feel that in this one case, it was entirely justified. Some people were just too evil to go on existing in the world. Some people added nothing and only did harm.

To the surprise of everyone gathered in the court, the prosecution called one final witness to testify to Rodney's character before he was sentenced. Tali Shapiro had not been seen or heard throughout any of Rodney's previous arrests or trials, she had not even been present in the country for the majority of his crimes and his trials, but now four decades after he had done the most unimaginable, awful things to her, she had found the strength to face him. She sat up on the stand and looked down at Rodney, and throughout it all, he could not meet her gaze. The man incapable of shame was uncomfortable.

She talked about what it was like to be his victim, how charming he could be, and the way that he talked girls into going with him, following him to somewhere secluded where he could do whatever he pleased with them. She talked about the way that the jovial personality he presented was wiped away when lust took him over and his body seemed to move of its own volition to maim and violate.

He was every bit the monster that they had all feared beneath his mask of humanity, and the testimony of Tali Shapiro peeled that mask back to reveal his true nature to the world in a way that days upon days of testimony about his crimes could not. She had been one of the girls who was murdered. It was pure luck that had let her slip through death's fingers and awaken from her coma after Rodney beat her well beyond the point of compliance and far into the shadow of the valley of death. It was easy to look at him and see a man, but she showed them all that he was a monster.

In his defence, all that Rodney managed to muster was a paid expert witness. Richard Rappaport was a psychiatrist who was willing to testify on Rodney's behalf that borderline personality disorder would explain how he could have committed the murders, as had already been proven but could have done so with no memory of the events involved. It was a paper-thin excuse for his actions, even if there had been any truth in it. The prosecutor countered this quite simply by pointing to Rodney's long and awful history. He was a sexual predator who knew that what he was doing was wrong. If he didn't know that what he was doing was wrong, he would not have gone to such great lengths to cover up his crimes. There could be no question of insanity excusing Rodney Alcala's actions when they were premeditated to such an extreme degree that he was scouting out murder locations months ahead of time.

He was sentenced to death for his crimes. Death by lethal injection. A date for that execution was scheduled, but everyone present knew that it would be delayed by another round of pointless appeals on Rodney's part. He fully intended to run out the clock if he could. All of that was exactly as expected. What nobody could have expected was when he broke away from the guards and ran over to Tali Shapiro.

She stood her ground, which must have taken unbelievable courage, and she listened to him as he spoke, which must have taken unbelievable restraint. He told her that he was sorry. That he should never have done that to her. That she had not deserved it. That he had felt guilty about it every day since that day.

All evidence seemed to be contrary to this, given that he had gone on doing just as bad if not worse things in the immediate aftermath of their encounter. Tali listened as he pleaded for her forgiveness and gave him no answer. He had taken her childhood from her. Taken her whole life from her. She had to leave the country because of what he had done, and now at the end of his endless spree of awful crimes, he was coming to her and begging for forgiveness. It wasn't hers to give. There were too many dead girls left in his wake for any one of the living to forgive him. Particularly when it was only luck that had kept her on this side of the graveyard gates and not the other. She departed the courtroom in stoic silence after Rodney had been hauled away. The cameras of the press outside chattering as she emerged into the late afternoon sunshine. She still kept her own counsel even when pressed for comment by every reporter present.

The endless trials that he had forced the victims' families to live through, time after time, had finally come to their end. Or at least, that was how it first seemed.

On the other coast, the police had been building their case against Rodney in New York for the murders he had committed there. Authorities announced that they would no longer pursue Rodney Alcala because he was on death row after his third trial, but in spite of this, a 2011 Manhattan grand jury indicted him for the murders of Cornelia Crilley and Ellen Hover. His execution was delayed indefinitely so that he could be shipped across the country to stand trial for the charges being levelled against him. He was extradited to New York in June 2012.

At court in New York, he filed not-guilty pleas on both counts, but he didn't really have any sort of defence strategy for the cases against him. They had his DNA, they had samples from both of the victims, and they had all of the information that they'd spent about thirty years gathering to provide the prosecution with a watertight case. All that Rodney had on his side was a desire for everything to play out as slowly as possible. The longer that he was in court in New York, the less likely it was that he was going to be flown back to receive a lethal injection in California.

After the first session in court in December of the same year, Rodney could see the writing on the wall. There was no long delay to be wrung out of these criminal proceedings because they were going to be open and shut. Everyone knew that he was guilty, and there was nothing that he'd be able to say or do to introduce enough reasonable doubt into anyone's mind to make this engagement last as long as he needed it to. His plan had been to bounce back and forth between the different jurisdictions of the USA as more of his victims were discovered, using each trial as an excuse to travel somewhere new and interesting, while also delaying his death sentence. He might even have offered up the odd confession or pointed the police in the right direction if it had seemed like things were going too slow and there was a chance he might have to face the music at last. But with DNA evidence providing such airtight cases, he realised that the golden age of his delaying scams was at an end. Many courts weren't even bringing charges against people without DNA evidence at this point, so ubiquitous was trust in it.

So instead of doing everything that he could to squeeze a few extra weeks out of the New York legal system, he announced to the court that he was changing his plea in both murders to guilty so that he could return to California and fight his death penalty appeal. A process that would almost certainly buy him his survival for a lot longer than this waste of time.

If the guilty plea was meant to buy him any leniency when it came to sentencing, it failed. He was sentenced to life in prison by the judge, as the death penalty had not been an option in New York since 2007, then loaded directly back onto a plane to return to King's County California and the prison cell that awaited him on death row. He arrived "home" in January of 2013.

Despite having very little legal standing, his appeal was still accepted by the court, and he was given time to prepare his case. Primarily because once his sentence had been carried out, there was no possibility of an appeal later. He worked extensively with new lawyers, scraping through every detail of his case, trying to find any legal precedent that might protect him, or even provide the slightest possibility of escaping his fate.

Still, he was able to delay the inevitable, and go on delaying the inevitable, until one day in July of 2021, at the age of 77, when the guards came to check on him first thing in the morning and they found that he was unresponsive. He was immediately transferred to a hospital in King's County where he remained comatose, but still watched over by an armed guard, until at 1:43 am on July 24th, 2021, he finally passed away.

Given his age, myriad existing health problems, and the lack of anyone demanding answers, no post-mortem examination was carried out, and as such the cause of his death was never discovered. There were a half dozen various ailments that he had acquired in his latter years, any one of which could have been the cause of death. If he had someone to advocate for him, perhaps the truth of what had finally finished him off would have come out, but the whole world was ready to forget Rodney Alcala by this point. He was a sordid and vile footnote in history that everyone was glad had finally come to a full stop.

At last, the story of one of the worst serial killers in American history had come to an end. Or at least, that was how it should have come to an end. All of his victims laid to rest, the monster lurking in the shadows dead, peace on earth. But it wasn't even close to over.

One Thousand and Twenty Photographs

The evidence that had been discovered in Rodney Alcala's locker in Seattle was continually examined in the years following his arrest. There were so many hundreds of different people photographed. Some casual snaps that he'd deigned to hold onto and intermingle with his trophies, and some sexually explicit pictures that had clearly been taken during the many rapes he had committed.

In 2010, the Huntington Beach and New York police departments worked in tandem to release one hundred and twenty of the photographs to the public, with the remaining 900 considered to be too explicit to disclose. They wanted to know the identity of anyone in the pictures. They wanted to know if there was anyone that had survived being Rodney Alcala's model unscathed.

Within the first few weeks, 21 women came forward to identify themselves. Women whom he had gone through the same routine as he had used to pick out his victims, but who he had inexplicably decided to allow to live. Some of them told tales of the pressure that he had put on them to engage in sexual activity with him, others told of entirely professional encounters resulting in pictures that they were able to add to their portfolios when seeking modelling work. The criteria by which Rodney decided who would live and who would die were entirely unclear. They were all added to the timeline of his activities, and it couldn't even be asserted that these 21 women were saved by some sort of scheduling. Many of them were photographed during periods when Rodney was not known to have taken any victims, and many of them had nobody who would have missed them if they had vanished at the time. It was as though Rodney had no logic to his actions at all. That the ones who had lived and those who had died had been chosen with the toss of a coin.

In addition to those women who had survived him, there were six other people identified in the pictures. People who had not been so lucky. Six different families came forward to identify a family member who had gone missing many years ago, disappearing without a trace and never being found. There had been no bodies of those victims discovered, if they were truly Rodney's victims and their disappearances were not coincidental. There was no way to prove that he had killed them now, regardless. Without a body, or a confession on his part, there was nothing that the police could do except list off the names of the missing in a file with Rodney's name on it and move on.

110 of the photos remain online to this day, as the police continue to solicit any further information, but it seems to be a dead end.

Yet despite the photographs leading nowhere, that was by no means the end of the investigation into the crimes of Rodney Alcala.

In March 2011, the police in Marin County, California announced that they had solved the case of Pamela Lambson. Pamela had been murdered in October of 1977 after being invited down to Fisherman's Wharf in San Francisco by a man who had offered to photograph her. It was Rodney's routine to a tee. Her body would later be discovered near a hiking trail north of the city, where she was found to have been beaten, stripped naked, and sexually assaulted. The police were confident enough in their assertion of Rodney's guilt that they were willing to announce it publicly, but there was no DNA evidence left on the body, nor were there any fingerprints. Without either of these, there was only the timeline, which fit perfectly, and the modus operandi, which matched the way that Rodney killed during that time period perfectly. Everything about the case screamed that it was the work of the "Dating Game Killer", but they could not legally pursue the matter further, considering doing so to be a waste of time, given that any extra charges added onto Rodney's sentence would be rendered moot by his death sentence.

Pamela had been 19 years old at the time of her death, matching perfectly with the bell curve of victim ages that Rodney was following throughout the 1970s. Everything added up.

In 2013, the photographs that the New York and Huntington Beach police departments had released finally secured their first hit. The picture was of a dark-haired woman in a yellow top riding on a motorcycle, a woman who was identified as Christine Thornton by her sister.

Christine had moved away from her family to live in San Antonio, Texas with her lover, but in June of 1977 when they were in Biloxi, Mississippi, the couple broke up. Poor Christine had travelled hundreds of miles to be with him, without any promise of marriage, on the basis of pure trust, and now she was entirely alone in the world without a penny to her name or anyone to help her. A matter that was exacerbated by the fact that she was now six months pregnant. She knew nobody in Biloxi, and without any means of contacting her family, she resorted to hitchhiking in any direction that she could. If she ended up back in Texas, she could pick up with the friends that she'd made there, and maybe they'd be able to help her get home to her family if she was going the other way, then all she could hope was that she'd get close enough to some member of her extended family and that they hadn't completely disowned her after she took off across the country.

She was never seen alive again. Someone picked her up. Someone murdered her too, eventually dumping her body off the side of Interstate 80 in Sweetwater, Wyoming. Her body would lay there until it was discovered in 1982, and would not be identified as hers until 2015 when her family managed to supply a DNA sample for matching to tissue samples from her remains.

Rodney quite readily admitted to taking the photograph, but denied killing the woman, despite the disposal of the body matching his usual behaviour perfectly. Even though the state of Wyoming proceeded with their plans to prosecute him on the basis of the scant evidence that they had in 2016, it was announced that Rodney Alcala's health was too fragile for him to make the journey and stand trial. By this point, he was 73 years old, and increasingly frail with each passing day. While he did not pass away for another four years, it would have been entirely unsurprising if that particular journey had finished him off.

As a more complete picture of Rodney's movements throughout the years was constructed, more and more cold cases were reopened. He was marked as a person of interest in several unsolved murders in California, New York, New Hampshire, and Arizona. In addition, since it was known that he frequented Seattle and Washington State thanks to his storage locker, the local police departments there began attempting to match his usual patterns of criminal behaviour to outstanding unsolved murders.

On September 14th, 1976, Cherry Ann Greenman was released from Douglas County Jail. It is assumed that Rodney picked her up when she was hitchhiking shortly afterwards. Because she was estranged from her family as a result of her criminal behaviour and adventurous lifestyle, her absence wasn't immediately noted but the fact that she had failed to make contact with anyone in her family soon became a cause for concern. She might not have been a part of their day-to-day life anymore, but regular check-ins were both normal and expected. Even in jail, she had been able to stay in touch, yet now that she had been released, there was not a sound?

As a result of the lifestyle that Cherry enjoyed, it took quite some time for the police to be convinced that she was actually missing and not simply itinerant. She was a traveller and explorer by nature, travelling across the United States as she pleased, making friends wherever she went and taking part-time work where she could find it. Whether that was seasonal farming or odd jobs about town. Yet throughout all of her travels and experiences, the one constant had always been the phone calls that she made home, to share stories of what she had been up to, and to keep up to date on all the comings and goings of her family.

As convinced as the Greenmans were that Cherry was missing, the police could not be convinced that someone failing to make a phone call constituted a missing person. At best, it made them a little bit rude. It was 2004 before the police would finally acknowledge that Cherry had vanished without a trace the same day she'd left their custody, and even that admission came only after the family had been making extensive enquiries of their own.

There was only one tiny piece of evidence as to where she might have disappeared. One clue that might have pointed the family in the right direction to finally find out what had happened to her on the fateful night of September 14th. In Rodney's locker in Seattle, the police had found a photograph of her.

At first, the cases were not connected, but eventually, as the investigators sifted through an endless heap of missing persons reports, trying to match them up to Rodney's collection of photographs, one of the investigators came to believe that Cherry was the subject in one of Rodney's pictures. Unfortunately, examining the most recent photograph that the state held of

Cherry and comparing it to the photo from Rodney's collection did not provide them with the unequivocal confirmation that they needed. They were going to need expert eyes to make the judgement.

Cherry's family travelled to Washington State to look at the photograph for themselves. The whole family was brought in together, walking silently through the halls of the police station, and shuffled into one of the interrogation rooms, where that single photograph lay face up in the middle of the table. Her mother picked it up and looked at it, before handing it along. Then her father. The whole family had come along so that they could support each other if the worst came to pass, or so they could confer if there was any doubt.

One by one they studied the picture, passing it back and forth inside the cellophane envelope meant to prevent any damage to the evidence. The picture made a circuit of the room before ending up back on the table, then Cherry's mother picked it up again and stared at it. Time seemed to grind to a halt as she made her decision, but finally, she announced that it wasn't Cherry.

Immediately, all of the family members rushed to agree with her, pointing out small details that, while insignificant to the investigators, told them with certainty that it wasn't Cherry that they were looking at. Sure she looked like Cherry, but that didn't mean she was Cherry. That didn't mean that Cherry, their little diamond in the rough, free spirit, roaming across the world had found her journey coming to an abrupt end at the hands of a serial killer who tortured his victims to death. It wasn't her. They didn't accept that it was her. They got quite agitated about the fact that the police had even suggested it. Their Cherry wouldn't have gone off with some strange man. Their Cherry wouldn't have let him take her picture. Their Cherry wouldn't have been strangled and revived over and over as Rodney Alcala raped her and beat her and snapped pictures for his own amusement. This was not their Cherry, and that was the story that they were sticking to.

As a result of this failure to identify Cherry in the picture, Rodney was never charged with the crime of killing her, and no further information about the woman could be found. She remains missing to this day, with an open call for any information regarding her location to be found on the Doe Network International Center For Unidentified and Missing Persons website and an open case file with the King's County Major Crimes Unit.

On the night of July 9, 1977, Antoinette "Tony" Jean Whittaker walked out of the foster home that she had been living in with a man who perfectly matched the description of Rodney Alcala. She was 13 years old, precocious in her interactions with older men, and that was the last time that she was seen alive.

Her absence was reported by her foster parents, but the general assumption was that she had run away from home with her new boyfriend. An assumption shared by both the foster parents and the police who did very little in the way of investigation after taking the initial witness statements.

A week later, a dead body was discovered in a vacant lot in the 2200 block of Northeast Street, Seattle. The body belonged to a 13-year-old girl who appeared to have died about a week beforehand. She was fully clothed, showed no signs of sexual assault, and had been killed by a knife wound. None of these disparate elements seemed to correspond to the usual way in which Rodney killed or disposed of bodies, but one peculiar element did tie them together despite all of the differences.

When Rodney killed and did not dispose of the bodies by simply dumping them out of his car like trash, he liked to pose the bodies in a very specific way. The bodies would be carefully placed down on their hands and knees. As though they were supplicants presenting themselves before him. It was not a detail that had ever been released to the press, and it was one of the ways that the various murders that Rodney had committed could be tied together despite the different ways in which he would kill.

Tony had been posed in the same way, and even though nothing else in the case seemed to match up, that was enough to put Rodney Alcala on the radar.

The case was never officially connected with Alcala beyond the cold case investigations noting those similarities and no charges were ever brought against him. Despite all of these oddities, there were many who have studied his crimes that firmly believe Tony Whittaker was one of Rodney's victims. Rodney had been known to use a knife in rare situations where he needed to kill his victims quickly and quietly. For instance, if he was dealing with one of them in a heavily populated area and needed to keep them quiet.

The lack of sexual assault and the fact that she remained clothed are the main roadblocks to a real connection between the killer and the case, but it is not impossible to imagine a scenario in which he attempted his usual rape and was surprised that the teenager fought back against him. Given their close proximity to bystanders – something that he was not accustomed to, given that he usually controlled the environment in which he processed his victims – he may very well have panicked and attempted to silence her as quickly as possible resulting in her remaining fully clothed, unviolated, and stabbed with all haste.

Despite this potential connection, the team working the cold case were never able to secure any solid evidence connecting Rodney to the crime. The description of the man who had picked up Tony had matched his description and he was assumed to have been in the area at the time when she died, but there was not enough in those things to constitute the foundations of a case. To this day, the murder remains unsolved.

Joyce Gaunt was 17 years old when she died, which may make it seem that she was perhaps more worldly and experienced than Tony Whittaker, but she was developmentally disabled, with the kind of intelligence one would connect with someone markedly younger. She had left the group home on Capitol Hill where she had been staying to meet with an unidentified man at Seward Park, where her body was discovered. She was arranged face-down in a picnic area, where it was almost certain that she would be discovered, and like most of Rodney's victims, she was found completely nude with signs of a violent beating and rape. There were also indications on the body that she had been repeatedly strangled to the point of death, and then allowed time to recover before her killer repeated the action again and again. Yet unlike Rodney's usual routine, it was not the asphyxiation that had resulted in her death, but a single heavy blow to the back of the head with a blunt object. Whatever that blunt object was remains a mystery, but it seems likely to have been a rock found nearby given the shape of the injury. She was discovered the day after she went missing on February 18th, 1978. Shortly before Rodney's television appearance.

None of these three murders were conclusively proven to have been the actions of Rodney Alcala, but there was sufficient circumstantial evidence in each case to make it seem plausible that he was responsible for their deaths. In combination with the many photographs that had been discovered in his locker that were later linked to missing people, it seems extremely likely that the murders for which he was convicted formed only a tiny percentage of the victims that he had actually taken.

Authorities believe that despite the official number of victims tied to Alcala numbering only eight, it is entirely possible that he was responsible for over one hundred and thirty killings.

This number was reached not based solely on the photographs and other evidence recovered from his locker, but also on the pattern of missing people that seemed to follow wherever he was located at a certain point in time. When he lived in New York, people vanished at a much higher rate in New York. When he was in California, their missing persons reports went through the roof. The exact number of victims that he took over the years is impossible to determine, but even accounting for the work of other serial killers that we know were operating at the same time, and the usual turnover of missing people in the respective areas where he travelled, it is quite likely possible that Rodney Alcala was one of the most prolific serial murderers in American history.

Henry Lee Lucas had long been considered the most prolific serial killer in US history, having confessed to six hundred murders. However, he would later recant many of these confessions, and even the ones that he did not recant were often dubious, to say the least. He was a man inclined to lying and he had greatly enjoyed being toured around the country and treated like a celebrity in exchange for claiming any unsolved murders in a jurisdiction. While this was initially a delight for the police, who used Lucas to clear their immense backlog of unsolved murders, it did not take long before he began tripping over his own lies, claiming to have travelled at supernatural speed from one side of the country to the other so that he could have committed a killing on one coast and then on the other the very next day. Before long, every single confession that Lucas had made was treated with doubt and suspicion and while officers of the law who benefitted the most from his false confessions did uphold that he may have killed two hundred, the fact remains that he was only ever convicted of four murders despite his best efforts to be connected to more. As such, Rodney, who was actively trying to conceal his killings is very likely to have surpassed him in terms of body count, much less in terms of the sheer number of lives irrevocably altered or ruined.

The pictures taken from Rodney's locker remain available to view online for the most part. The most sexually explicit, and those which are sexually explicit and feature a minor, have been withheld from the public for obvious reasons. Discounting those victims who have already been identified from the pictures being shown, and those who can be directly connected to a now-solved murder, there are still literally hundreds of people from those photographs that remain unaccounted for.

Is it likely that he killed all of the people in the pictures? Of course not. We have testimony from many of his models stating that more often than not, the pictures were the reward in themselves and that Rodney was actively trying to build a real portfolio so that he could continue to find photography work in the fashion and glamour industry. Yet that does not explain why not all of the people in those pictures have come forward to identify themselves. Even if there was some degree of shame involved, particularly considering the rather sordid nature of many of the pictures, surely common decency would have demanded that they step up and remove themselves from the list of possible victims. The very fact that so many of those photographed remain entirely unidentified suggests that something happened to them that prevented them from coming forward. Not to mention the fact that the only thing that Rodney kept in that locker beyond his collection of photographs were trophies that he had taken from his victims.

Two murders he committed were linked to earrings found in a pouch in his storage locker, but there were many more earrings in that pouch, earrings in the style women wore when Rodney was actively raping and killing. Dozens of earrings that suggested he was involved in many more murders than were proven against him in court.

It's highly improbable that he killed all the people in the pictures. But that does not mean that he didn't kill some or even most of them. The fact that so many of them remain unidentified and unaccounted for suggests that something happened to them that would prevent them from coming forward. And, of course, there are long periods of time during his killing spree where there are simply no records of victims. Does it seem likely that a man with appetites like Rodney Alcala would simply ignore his darkest impulses for months at a time when he could not even resist abducting a little girl after being seen by her and all of her friends taking their picture?

The sad fact is that the people in the photographs will remain anonymous. We will never know what happened to all of his models, whether they lived or died, whether they achieved their dreams of celebrity or met an untimely end at the hands of a serial killer, their bodies dumped somewhere so remote that they still haven't been found, or lost for long enough that when their remains were recovered there was no way of knowing who the desiccated bones had belonged to. There was only one person who connected all of the people in those photographs, all of the young boys, girls, and women who had been convinced to strip bare before the camera of a psychopath, and that one person is now dead.

Even before he passed on, Rodney never showed any signs of remorse, beyond his brief apology in court to Tali Shapiro. He never made apologies to the families of the women that he killed, he never provided the police with the details that they would need to put other missing people to rest and relieve their families of the burden of wondering what had happened to their loved ones. Why would he? He didn't care about any of them, any more than he had cared about the people that he had used as toys and discarded once he had broken them. The same sickness inside of him that had allowed him to commit these atrocious acts for his sadistic sexual satisfaction meant that he would never feel enough compassion to put himself at risk of further punishment. To the very end, he clung onto the husk of his life with both hands, refusing to help anyone that he had hurt, until finally it was too late.

The true monstrosity of Rodney Alcala was that he had never been capable of seeing them as people from the very beginning. He may not have derived pleasure from killing them in the way that other serial killers did, but in a way that made him even more monstrous. To most serial killers, murder is a compulsion, murder is the only way that they can find release.

For Rodney, it was simply a way of disposing of a problem. For all that he was driven by his passions to commit terrible crimes, the actual murders were perpetrated entirely in cold blood as acts of necessity rather than passion.

With many serial killers, it is relatively easy to spot the exact point that their lives veered off the tracks. A traumatic head injury, an abusive parent, a catastrophic tragedy. Something so violent and powerful that their whole psyche was disassembled, and they had to try to piece it back together again but they failed to make themselves whole. With Rodney, however, it seems as though there was no instigating incident that transformed him from a normal child into the abusive, manipulative sociopath that he became. Unlike so many cases where these monsters were created by some dark twist of fate, with Rodney, there was just a gradual progression. The awkward teenager manufactured his own trauma in the form of rejection and then used it to justify doing what he had wanted to do all along, take sex with force instead of consent.

An argument could be made that his somewhat tumultuous early life, with repeated moves and his parent's divorce, may have contributed in some way to Rodney's psychopathy, but considering that nearly half of all marriages in America end in divorce yet the place is not overrun by juvenile serial killers and rapists, we are led to the unfortunate conclusion that Rodney Alcala was simply born wrong. Something in his physiology and psychology was fundamentally different from the people around him and this difference deprived Rodney of any sense of morality.

As previously mentioned, the dark trinity of a serial killer's psychology consists of psychopathy, narcissism and sadism. Psychopaths are born all the time. It is not a particularly common genetic condition, but neither is it nearly as uncommon as people believe. The world has a sizeable proportion of people who are incapable of empathy, driven exclusively by the desire to get whatever they can for themselves. Many of these people end up as CEOs, lawyers, and surgeons, people who benefit from not having to feel what those they work with feel and who make decisions based exclusively on pure logic as they perceive it. They can be unsettling to people with the typical mental makeup, but they are by no means dangerous.

Likewise, there are a great many narcissists who believe that they are the most important person in the world, selfish to the ultimate extreme and driven to centre themselves in everything that is going on, but they too are not dangerous, except in the sense that other people can end up trapped in their emotional manipulation.

Last, and perhaps most importantly, there are the sexual sadists. On paper that would seem to be the most dangerous of the trifecta of serial killer traits. People who derive sexual pleasure from doing harm to others sound terrifying. In reality, however, the overwhelming majority of sexual sadists practice their proclivities in privacy, with consenting partners. The idea of the sadist roaming the streets in search of someone to maim is ridiculously farcical. Given the number of sexual masochists in the world, who derive pleasure from experiencing some degree of pain, the sexual sadist is actually in great demand. They can find numerous partners within the communities built around these sexual practices and would, therefore, never feel any need to roam beyond their circle of similarly-minded individuals.

The combination of two of these traits might produce an unpleasant person to be around, but it is only when all three occur together that you typically see a serial killer emerge, and even when all three of the traits occur in a single person, it is no guarantee that they will become violent in later life. This psychological trifecta can help to predict when a person is capable of becoming a serial killer with some degree of accuracy, but it does not guarantee it. The majority of people with a combination of all three of these traits never commit a single act of violence in their adult lives because, ultimately, it is easier for them to blend into society and experience all of its benefits rather than working at cross-purposes. We live in a world that suits psychopaths, narcissists, and sadists very comfortably, a series of systems that seems like it was designed to benefit them, if truth be told. So why would they throw all of that away for the quick thrill of murder?

There is a fourth trait that has not been identified or validated by science. It is the aspect of a serial killer that drives them to commit the heinous acts that they commit. A trait that many would call evil. And that trait was incontrovertibly present in Rodney Alcala. If anything, it was his defining trait, even more so than sadism, psychopathy, or narcissism.

Whatever made Rodney Alcala into the person that he was, the reality of the situation is that if he were not arrested when he was, there would have been considerably more dead bodies to be found. Whether you believe that he was only responsible for the deaths that he was charged and indicted for, or whether you believe that every single photograph in his collection represents a different victim, the fact remains that if he had not been arrested and locked away from society, he would have continued to kill again and again. There was never any remorse in him, and it was clear that whatever drove him to rape and kill was not going to abate.

Rodney Alcala benefitted greatly from a system of justice that was built on the idea of reformation and rehabilitation. The idea that taking a criminal and placing them into a prison or mental institution would somehow transform them from the worst kind of monster into a functioning member of society is myopic, at best.

All that Rodney had to do was perform some act of compliance and he could be set free. Free to kill and rape and torture all over again. He is a case study of why prisons actually exist. Some people cannot be reformed. They cannot change and become good people. They are criminals, not due to circumstances or quirks of psychology, but because they are evil. The purpose of a prison is not to try and mend this person, or even to punish them. The purpose of prison for a man like Rodney Alcala is to contain him. To prevent him from hurting other people. It is impossible to instil morals in such a person, impossible to change their mind about whether their crimes were worth the punishment. As intelligent as he was, it never once seemed to occur to Rodney that he could simply choose not to kill.

Once he had started down that path, it seemed he couldn't conceive of any way to get off it. More importantly, he didn't want to.

We often view serial killers as something like a force of nature, shaped by circumstances into living weapons that wreak havoc because they were made into monsters that are simply wrapped in human skin, but the fact of the matter is that they are human. In Rodney's case, he was just as human as anyone else. When confronted with the choice to either do something truly evil that might bring him pleasure or to choose not to, he chose the selfish option. He chose it again and again.

With glee in his heart, Rodney went out hunting for a new girl to rape and torture. With every lie that he told and every person that he manipulated for the sole purpose of making his life easier, he was choosing the same course over and over again. His life was not a predetermined course that he was helpless to alter once he'd started moving forward. His path was a long sequence of choices between doing the right thing and doing the wrong thing, and he chose to do the wrong thing every single time. Not because of some compulsion resulting from a warped or shattered psyche, but because he was presented with different options and he chose to do what he thought that he would enjoy the most, regardless of what it cost other people.

Psychopathy is often considered to be the selfish impulses in all of us taken to an extreme, but even most psychopaths would never even consider doing the things that Rodney did. He had no excuse, he had no reason, all that he had was a desire that he acted on with reckless abandon, slaughtering anyone that he thought might interfere with his future pleasure.

He was a child molester before all else, choosing his victims carefully to ensure that they would never be strong enough to put up any real fight. Even when he selected older victims, it was never anyone who might have presented a challenge.

There is another mythos surrounding serial killers – that they are like predators, tracking prey and overcoming them through skill and strength. The reality could not have been further from the truth, at least in this case. Rodney found people who were unable to defend themselves almost at random, repeated the same script that he'd found to be successful early in his adult life and sometimes managed to muster up just enough courage to go through with the rape and murder that he wanted to engage in every time he took somebody's picture. In that way, perhaps the storage locker filled with pictures is not a testament to Rodney Alcala's massive number of victims, but a monument to his cowardice. He wanted to hurt other people all the time, and he never resisted that urge when he felt certain he could get away with it without any risk to himself and his comfort, but the rest of the time, he chose not to kill, not to rape, not to torture, because he did not have the courage of his convictions.

For all that he might have justified his crimes with some bloated sense of entitlement after his early teenage years had revolved around rejection, the fact of the matter was that he only went after those who were too weak to resist him. These were not the starlets in the making who wouldn't give him the time of day in high school, or even the girls hanging around the military base boys looking for a good time. They were innocent children, the disabled, and the isolated. People who he would not have looked at twice when he was trying to pick up a date, but who simply became his prey because they were easy pickings.

Given the number of dead bodies left in his wake and the volume of potential victims that he has left behind, one might expect Rodney Alcala to have left a massive footprint on

American culture. You might expect him to be remembered in the same breath as serial killers like Bundy, Dahmer, or Gacy. For the most part, however, he has slipped into obscurity, despite having been alive until only a few years ago. There is nothing in his story that can be romanticised. There is nothing in his story that is enlightening. He was an intelligent man who chose to live like a savage animal. He was not worth remembering.

Yet despite the contempt and distaste that most hold for Alcala, there have been a few notable pieces of media following his story. A biographical film called the 'Dating Game Killer' appeared in 2017, at the height of the True Crime craze dominating television. In 2021 actress Anna Kendrick made her directorial debut with the film 'Woman of the Hour' revolving around Rodney's appearance on the Dating Game television show and in November of 2022, 'Dating Death,' a 3-part documentary series about Alcala was released.

Every one of these stories centred his appearance on the Dating Game as the most notable thing about him. He had killed perhaps a hundred or more people, but his five-minute appearance on television was all that made him interesting. Whether a testament to the shortsightedness of our mediacentric culture or a damning indictment of every other aspect of Rodney Alcala's life, it is remarkable that even as a prolific serial killer, he just wasn't capable of holding our attention.

SMILE

Want More?

Did you enjoy *Smile* and want some more True Crime?

YOUR FREE BOOK IS WAITING

From bestselling author Ryan Green

There is a man who is officially classed as "**Britain's most dangerous prisoner**"

The man's name is Robert Maudsley, and his crimes earned him the nickname "**Hannibal the Cannibal**"

This free book is an exploration of his story...

★★★★★ *"Ryan brings the horrifying details to life. I can't wait to read more by this author!"*

Get a free copy of **Robert Maudsley: Hannibal the Cannibal** when you sign up to join my Reader's Group.

www.ryangreenbooks.com/free-book

Every Review Helps

If you enjoyed the book and have a moment to spare, I would really appreciate a short review on Amazon. Your help in spreading the word is gratefully received and reviews make a huge difference to helping new readers find me. Without reviewers, us self-published authors would have a hard time!

Type in your link below to be taken straight to my book review page.

US	geni.us/SmileUS
UK	geni.us/SmileUK
Australia	geni.us/SmileAUS
Canada	geni.us/SmileCAN

Thank you! I can't wait to read your thoughts.

About Ryan Green

Ryan Green is a true crime author who lives in Herefordshire, England with his wife, three children, and two dogs. Outside of writing and spending time with his family, Ryan enjoys walking, reading and windsurfing.

Ryan is fascinated with History, Psychology and True Crime. In 2015, he finally started researching and writing his own work and at the end of the year, he released his first book on Britain's most notorious serial killer, Harold Shipman.

He has since written several books on lesser-known subjects, and taken the unique approach of writing from the killer's perspective. He narrates some of the most chilling scenes you'll encounter in the True Crime genre.

You can sign up to Ryan's newsletter to receive a free book, updates, and the latest releases at:

WWW.RYANGREENBOOKS.COM

More Books by Ryan Green

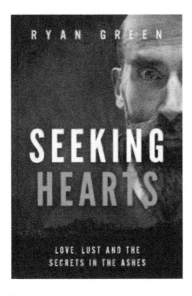

When Inspector Belin set out to catch the elusive Henri Landru for embezzlement and fraud, he wasn't prepared for the complex web of secrets that would unravel.

As war raged on and husbands fought on distant battlefields, Landru preyed upon the vulnerable hearts of lonely young women, presenting himself as a grieving widower desperate to fill the void in his shattered life.

Beneath the façade of a broken man lay a disturbing truth - a predator driven by insatiable desires. Would some of Landru's 283 targets find out in time to save themselves?

Seeking Hearts is a chilling journey through the depths of human darkness. As the riveting tale unfolds, it forces readers to confront the unsettling realisation that, for Henri Landru, murder became the ultimate means of tying up loose ends.

More Books by Ryan Green

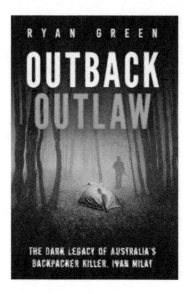

"He was going to kill somebody from the age of 10. It was built into him... I knew he was on a one-way trip. I knew that it was just a matter of how long." - Boris Milat, Ivan's brother

Detaining a man like Ivan Milat would be a monumental challenge. His obsession with firearms and hatred of state power were a highly volatile combination. Sending just a couple of men would result in two dead officers and a prime suspect on the run.

Outback Outlaw is an unflinching and uncompromising account of a man forever cemented in the annals of Australian true crime. Ryan Green's riveting narrative draws the reader into the real-life horror experienced by the victim and has all the elements of a classic thriller.

More Books by Ryan Green

On the bloodstained floor lay an array of butcher's tools and a body without a throat, torn out by Fritz's "love bite"...

Deemed psychologically unfit to stand trial for child abuse, Fritz Haarmann was locked up in a mental asylum until a new diagnosis as "morally inferior" allowed him to walk free. His insights into the criminal underworld convinced the police to overlook his "activities" and trust him as an informant.

What harm could it do?

When the dismembered and ravaged remains of young men began to wash up on the banks of the river, a war-torn nation cowered under the threat of the man known as the Butcher, Vampire and Wolf Man.

The hunt for the killer was on, and he was hiding in plain sight.

More Books by Ryan Green

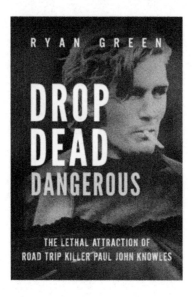

In 1974, the US East Coast was whipped up into a frenzy of fear. Locking their windows and doors, everyone was terrified of becoming the next victim of the strikingly handsome but deadly "*Casanova Killer*". And he was on the move.

After being released from jail and promptly abandoned by his fiancée, Paul John Knowles embarked on a spate of gruesome murders on a road trip up the Pacific Coast.

No room for fear, no room for guilt, just the road

As the man-hunt gathered pace, the cold-blooded killing spree continued to defy detectives. With no visible pattern in the age, race nor gender of the victims, Knowle's joyride of kidnap, rape and murder tore across multiple state borders. It became a race of tragically high stakes. How many more lives would be lost before the police finally caught up.

Free True Crime Audiobook

Sign up to Audible and use your free credit to download this collection of twelve books. If you cancel within 30 days, there's no charge!

WWW.RYANGREENBOOKS.COM/FREE-AUDIOBOOK

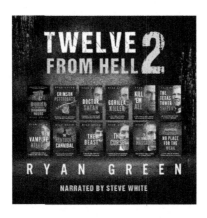

"Ryan Green has produced another excellent book and belongs at the top with true crime writers such as M. William Phelps, Gregg Olsen and Ann Rule" –**B.S. Reid**

"Wow! Chilling, shocking and totally riveting! I'm not going to sleep well after listening to this but the narration was fantastic. Crazy story but highly recommend for any true crime lover!" –**Mandy**

"Torture Mom by Ryan Green left me pretty speechless. The fact that it's a true story is just...wow" –**JStep**

"Graphic, upsetting, but superbly read and written" –**Ray C**

WWW.RYANGREENBOOKS.COM/FREE-AUDIOBOOK

Printed in Great Britain
by Amazon